CHARMING SMALL HOTEL GUIDES

NEW ENGLAND

AND NEW YORK CITY

CHARMING SMALL HOTEL GUIDES

NEW ENGLAND

AND NEW YORK CITY

EDITED BY

Paul Wade & Kathy Arnold

DUNCAN PETERSEN

This new 2005 edition
conceived, designed and produced by
Duncan Petersen Publishing Ltd,
31 Ceylon Road, London W14 0YP

Conceived, designed and produced by
Duncan Petersen Publishing Ltd,

Editorial director Andrew Duncan
Editors Paul Wade, Kathy Arnold
Principal inspector Lans Christensen
Additional inspectors Tom Arnold, Robert Baram, Ron and Janet Evans,
Nancianne Henchcliffe, Gael May McKibben, Dorothy Segal
Production editors Sarah Boyall and Sophie Page
Art editor Don Macpherson
Production Sarah Hinks

Sales representation and distribution in the U.K. and Ireland by
Portfolio Books Ltd
Unit 5, Perivale Industrial Park
Horsenden Lane South
Greenford, UB6 7RL
Tel: 0208 997 9000 Fax: 0208 997 9097
E-mail: sales@portfoliobooks.com

A CIP catalogue record for this book is available
from the British Library

ISBN 1-903301-23-8

Typeset by Duncan Petersen Publishing Ltd
Printed by E.G Zure, Spain

CONTENTS

INTRODUCTION

Welcome to this new 3rd edition of *Charming Small Hotel Guides New England and New York City*.

Charming and small

In the USA, where giant hotels are the rule, popular demand for small, personally-run inns, hotels and bed-and-breakfasts shows no sign of diminishing. This updated edition of the guide to New England re-assesses old friends and introduces new ones. More and more visitors flock to this area, comprising the states of Maine and New Hampshire, Vermont and Massachusetts, Rhode Island and Connecticut, many landing in New York City. The last is included for that reason despite not being part of New England.

To Americans, New England means history. The region feels 'old' to Americans and familiar to Europeans, thanks to small towns and villages, historic houses and inns. These are the charming, small, family-run hotels and bed-and-breakfasts that epitomise the famous American hospitality.

Hotels, inns, and bed-and-breakfasts

Under the collective banner of Charming Small Hotels we list all sorts of accomodation: posh hotels, well-known restaurants with a few bedrooms, and bed-and-breakfasts. In New England most, however, call themselves 'inns'. In the USA, that word conjures up an image of a white clapboard house on a village green, with fireplaces and plenty of antiques inside. Colonial inns have the bare floor boards and muted colours of the 18th century; Victorian inns are full of patterned fabrics and dark wood. A few are even unashamedly modern. The welcome, however, should be personal and warm.

To Americans, therefore, a New England inn is more than just a place to stay the night: it is a special experience. "Ten years ago, people wanted to know if I had four-poster beds; then it was king-size beds; now it's Jacuzzis," one innkeeper told us. Demands are high; so are standards of comfort. Unlike country hotels in Europe, however, where telephones and televisions in bedrooms are taken for granted, many New England inns deliberately do not have them. In these places, the aim is to offer an escape from the frantic pace of modern life. That does not mean, however, that their prices are lower. Unfortunately, the word 'inn' has become a cliché: nowadays it is used for motels and also for hotels with 100 rooms. Our selections have around 25 bedrooms, some have fewer than ten. Even in New York City, most choices have no more than 60 rooms. Overall, they range from total luxury to honest simplicity

We give our opinions on furnishings, atmosphere, value for money and, most importantly, the welcome. We are not fans of trouser presses or mini-bars pre-stocked with expensive drinks; we prefer fresh flowers and a big smile.

This selection of hotels, inns and bed-and-breakfasts has been made after thorough research, personal recommendations and

So what exactly do we look for?

- *A peaceful, attractive setting in an interesting and picturesque position.*

- *A building that is either handsome or interesting or historic, or at least with a distinct character.*

- *Bedrooms that are well proportioned with as much character as the public rooms below.*

- *Ideally, we look for adequate space, but on a human scale: we don't go for places that rely on grandeur, or that have pretensions that could intimidate.*

- *Decorations must be harmonious and in good taste, and the furnishings and facilities comfortable and well maintained. We like to see interesting antique furniture that is there because it can be used, not simply revered.*

- *The proprietors and staff need to be dedicated and thoughtful, offering a personal welcome, without being intrusive. The guest needs to feel like an individual.*

expert assessment by a team of inspectors chosen by the editors. No establishment pays to be in this guide.

How to find an entry
Starting with New York City, we divide New England into four areas, starting with Southern, moving through Central to Northern and North-eastern New England. Each area has its own map, with hotel locations marked and page references.

Within each area are the states. The main, full-page entries are listed in alphabetical order by town. Finally come the shorter entries in area order, again listed in alphabetical order by town.

There are three easy ways to find a hotel:
- Use the maps between pages 10 and 31. The numbers on the map refer to the page in the book where the hotel is listed.
- If you know the area you want to visit, browse through that section until you find a place that fits the bill.
- Use the indexes at the back, which list entries both by hotel name (p186-188) and by location (p189-192).

Entries
As in other books in the series, our warmest recommendations are given in full-page reports, complete with colour photographs. At the back of the book is a further selection of shorter entries. These

have been inspected and are by no means 'second class' choices, but for one reason or another do not justify a full page.

Bedrooms
Four-poster and canopy beds are commonplace in New England inns. Sizes range from double, to queen and king but most inns also offer twin bedded rooms. 'Working fireplaces' are also popular; if you want one, expect to pay for the privilege. Many inns are converted old homes, so bedrooms come in all sizes; bathrooms are rarely spacious and can be tiny. Inns often refer to 'decks' (wooden balconies or terraces) and 'hot tubs' (deep, hot water baths for relaxation, not washing).

Meals
Breakfast may surprise first-time European visitors. Expect muffins and breads and often a 'special' of the day, perhaps pancakes or an egg dish. Breakfast may be served on a first-come, first-served basis or at a set time, at communal or separate tables. If you have strong feelings about how you start the day, be sure to check exactly what is on offer.

Your host and hostess
New England's innkeepers are enthusiastic: eager to relate the history of their home and to advise on local attractions.

Travel facts
The tourist information offices for each state are listed with the relevant maps a few pages further on.

New England is well-served via the international airports in Boston, New York and Montreal, plus a range of regional airports such as Bangor, ME, Burlington, VT, Hartford, CT, Manchester, NH, Portland, ME, and TF Green, Warwick/Providence, RI. Among the major airlines flying in to New England, Delta, with Delta Connection, has frequent services, both from within North America and from Europe. For reservations in USA, call (800) 221 1212; in the UK, call 0800 414767. Delta also operates an excellent website, www.delta.com.

How to read an entry
At the top of the page is the area of New England; below that is the state; then follows the type of hotel, its town and, finally, the name of the hotel itself.

Tel, fax, e-mail, website
The first number is the area code. The additional 800 and 888 area codes are for toll-free calls made in the USA.

Location
The setting of the hotel is described briefly; car parking facilities follow.

Prices

The range of prices is from the cheapest single room in low season to the most expensive double in high season.

$	up to $100 $
$$	$100 to $175 $$
$$$	$175 to $250 $$$
$$$$	over $250 $$$$

A few hotels have rooms only in one price band. Do ask proprietors about special 'packages' or reductions for length of stay. Some allow children to share a room; ask about the extra charge. Always confirm prices when making a reservation and check how much local state taxes and gratuities add to the cost.

Some inns provide dinner only for guests, others have restaurants open to the public. Few serve lunch. Most bed-and-breakfasts provide an afternoon snack for guests. Prices generally are in relation to the cost of bedrooms. For a 3-course meal for one person without wine, coffee, taxes or gratuities, expect to pay: from $25 in a $ hotel; from $30 in a $$ hotel; from $35 in a $$$ hotel; from $40 in a $$$$ hotel. Where dinner, bed and breakfast is obligatory (DB & B), the price quoted is the rate for one person per night.

Facilities

We list public rooms plus outdoor and sporting facilities. Public sports facilities and attractions near the hotel are under **Nearby**.

Smoking

Some hotels have a few rooms where smoking is allowed; most bed-and-breakfast inns are 'non-smoking' indoors.

Credit cards

We use the following abbreviations for credit cards:

    AE American Express
    DC Diners Club
    MC Master Card
    V Visa/Barclaycard/Bank Americard/Carte Bleue

Many inns accept credit cards reluctantly, preferring cash or travellers' cheques.

Children

While some inns welcome children, others are aimed at adults. [The age shown is our assessment of what is appropriate for that hotel. Always ask the innkeeper, however.]

Closed

It is important to check the exact dates of closing; bed-and-breakfasts, in particular, may close for a few weeks in off-season.

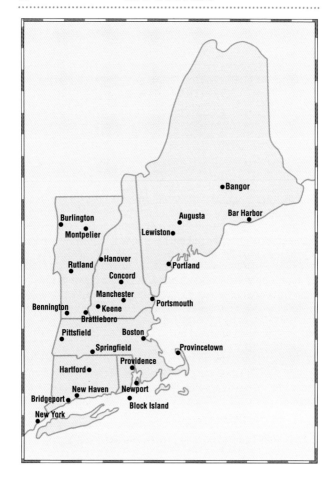

MAPS OF HOTEL LOCATIONS

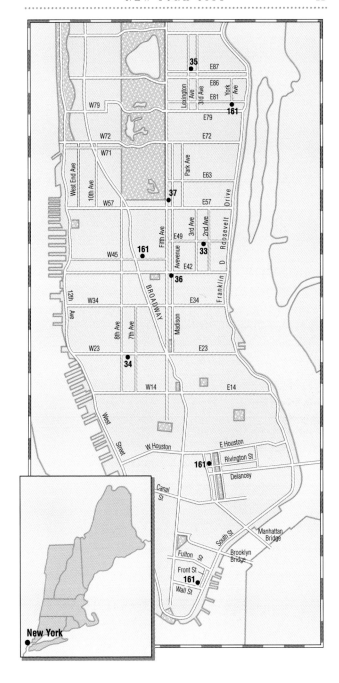

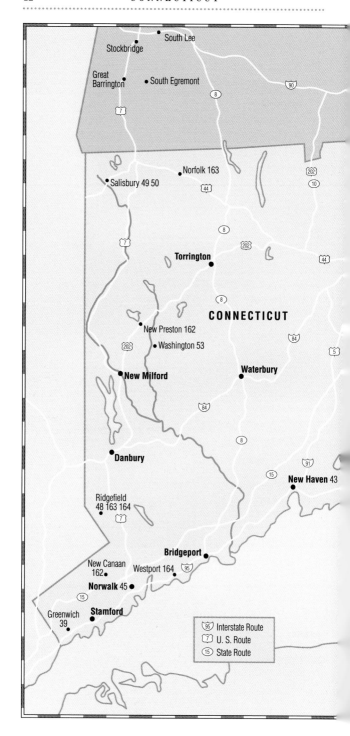

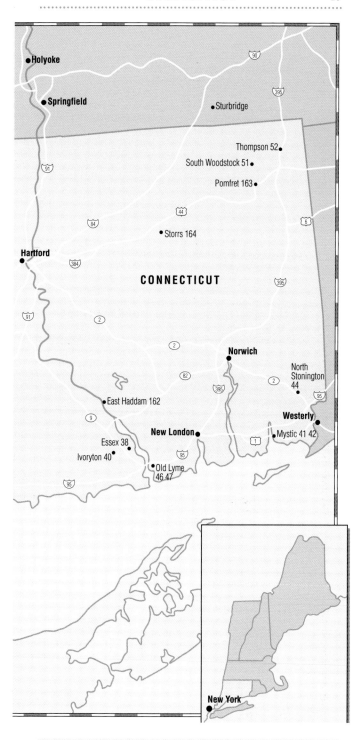

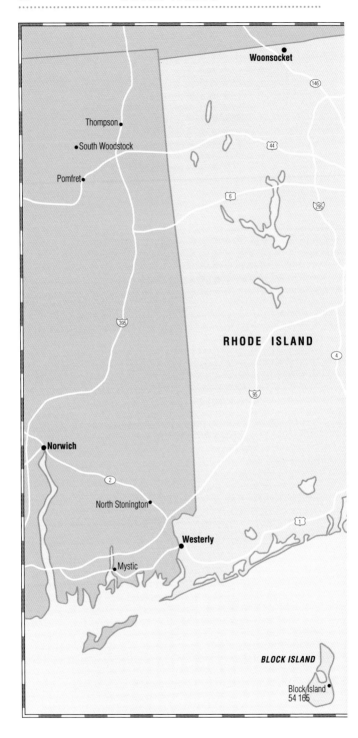

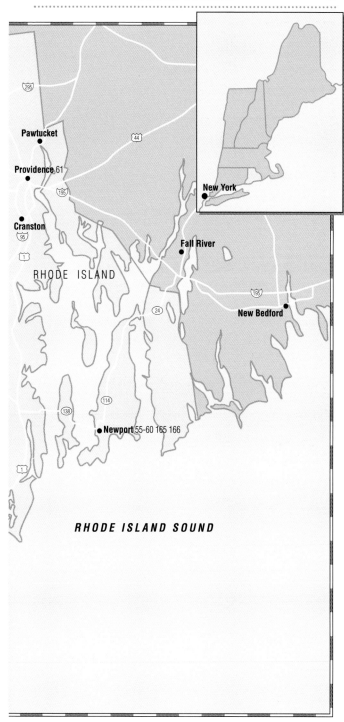

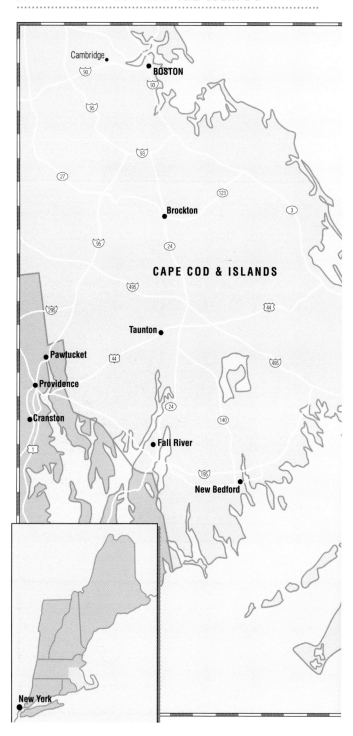

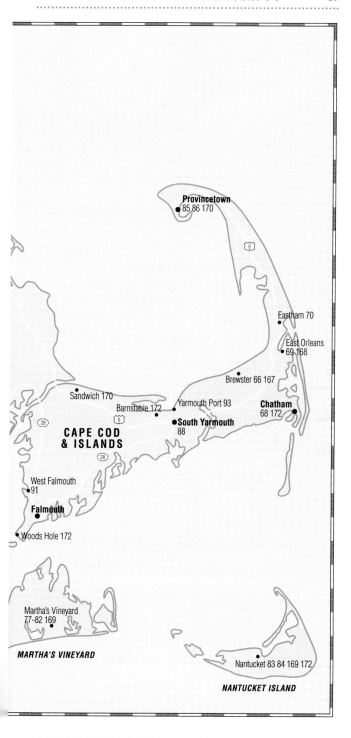

Provincetown
85 86 170

6

Eastham 70

East Orleans
69 168

Brewster 66 167

Sandwich 170

Barnstable 172   Yarmouth Port 93   **Chatham**
6   68 172

South Yarmouth
88

**CAPE COD
& ISLANDS**

28

West Falmouth
91

Falmouth

Woods Hole 172

Martha's Vineyard
77-82 169

MARTHA'S VINEYARD

Nantucket 83 84 169 172

NANTUCKET ISLAND

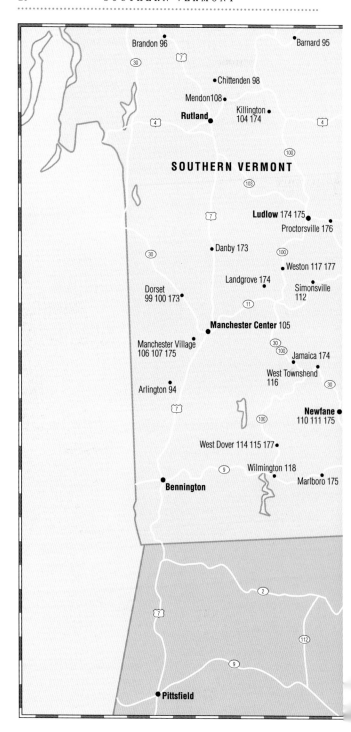

Brandon 96

Barnard 95

Chittenden 98

Mendon108

Killington
104 174

Rutland

SOUTHERN VERMONT

Ludlow 174 175

Proctorsville 176

Danby 173

Weston 117 177

Landgrove 174

Simonsville
112

Dorset
99 100 173

Manchester Center 105

Manchester Village
106 107 175

Jamaica 174

West Townshend
116

Newfane
110 111 175

Arlington 94

West Dover 114 115 177

Wilmington 118

Bennington

Marlboro 175

Pittsfield

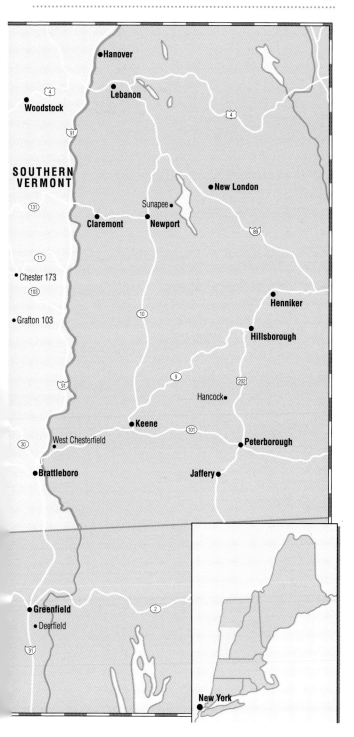

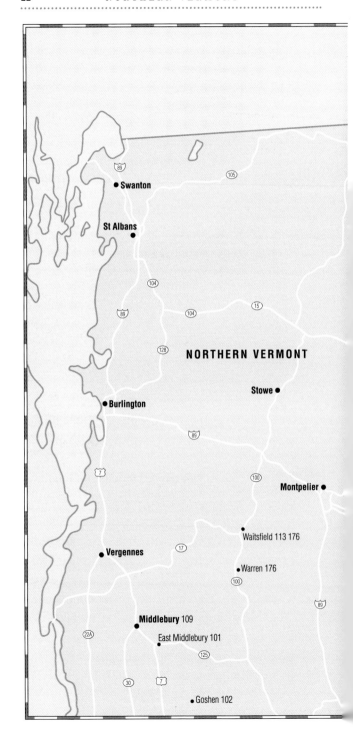

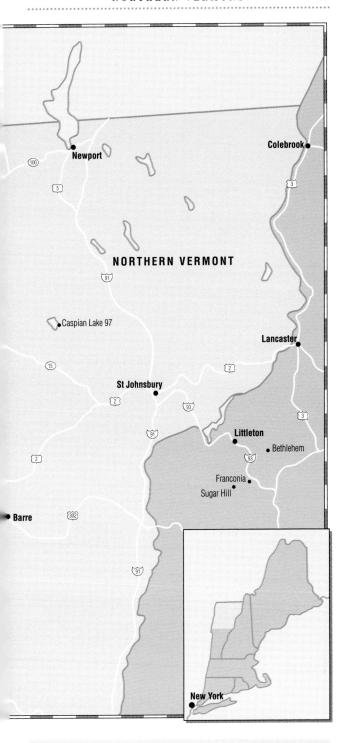

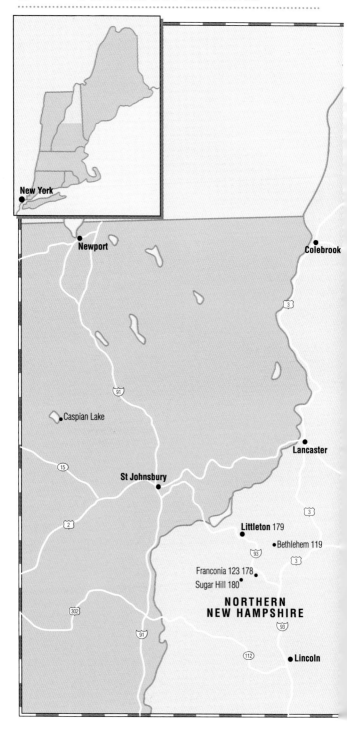

NORTHERN
NEW HAMPSHIRE

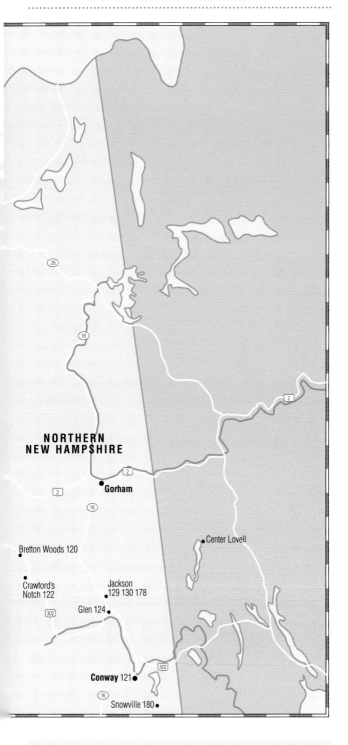

NORTHERN
NEW HAMPSHIRE

Gorham

Center Lovell

Bretton Woods 120

Jackson
129 130 178

Crawford's
Notch 122

Glen 124

Conway 121

Snowville 180

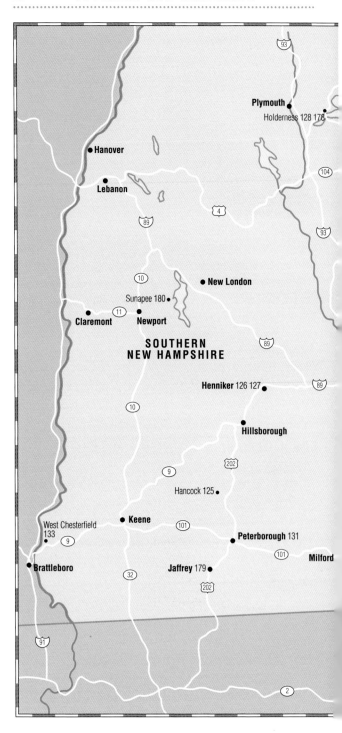

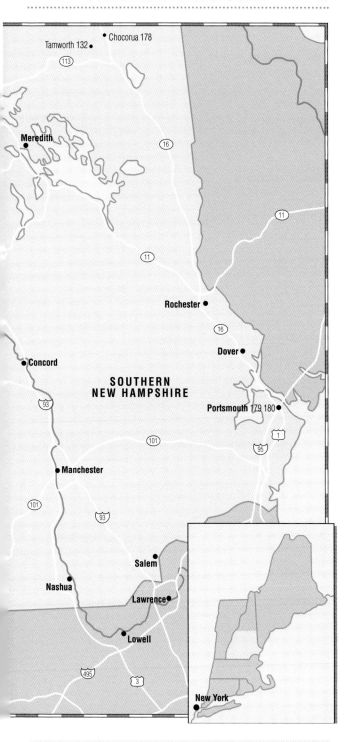

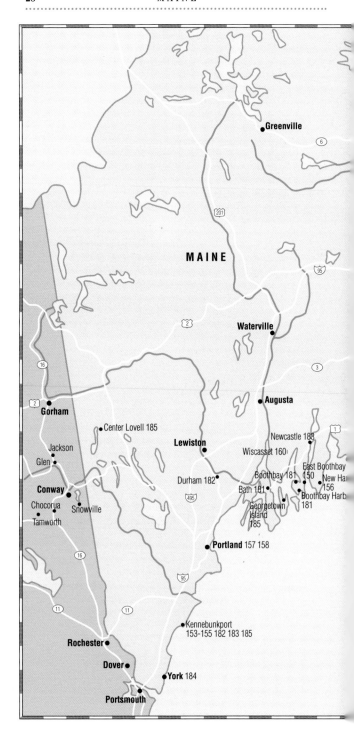

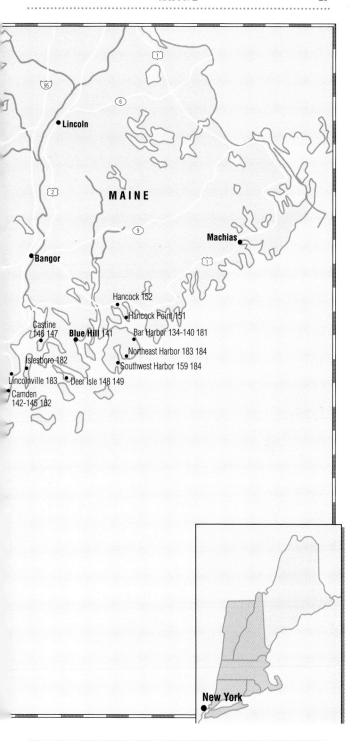

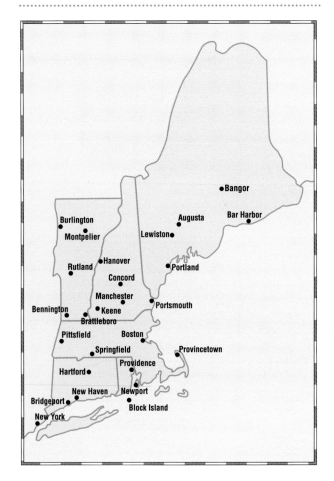

Travel Distances

Distances of some key towns from Boston

Boston to:	Miles	Boston to:	Miles
Albany, N.Y.	177	Montpelier, Vt.	201
Augusta, Maine	166	Montreal, Quebec	320
Bangor, Maine	230	New Bedford, Mass.	58
Bennington, Vt.	147	New Haven, Conn.	130
Bar Harbor, Maine	271	Newport, R.I.	72
Berlin, N.H.	176	New York, N.Y.	223
Brattleboro, Vt.	104	Pittsfield, Mass.(the Berkshires)	137
Bridgeport, Conn.	150	Portland, Maine	103
Burlington, Vt.	228	Portsmouth, N.H.	56
Concord, N.H.	67	Presque Isle, Maine	389
Hanover, N.H.	144	Providence, R.I.	43
Hartford, Conn.	93	Provincetown, Mass. (Cape Cod)	115
Keene, N.H.	86	Rutland, Vt.	164
Lewiston, Maine	138	Springfield, Mass.	83
Manchester, N.H. 4	9		

January
New Year's Day
Third Monday   Martin Luther King Jr Day (long weekend)

February
Second weekend   Lincoln's Birthday (long weekend)
Third weekend   Washington's Birthday (long
                        weekend)(Presidents' Week, linking the
                        two weekends, is often a school holiday)

March
First Tuesday   Town Meeting Day (Vermont)

April
Third Monday   Patriots' Day (Massachusetts and Maine,
                        long weekend)

May
Last weekend   Memorial Day (long weekend)

July
4th   Independence Day

August
Second Monday   Victory Day (Rhode Island long weekend)
16th   Bennington Battle Day (Vermont)

September
First Monday   Labor Day (long weekend)

October
Second Monday   Columbus Day (long weekend)

November
First Tuesday   Election Day (some states)
11th   Veterans Day
Fourth Thursday   Thanksgiving Day

December
25th   Christmas Day

Fall Foliage Hotlines
Each state runs a special hotline with up to the minute information
on the best places to see the fall colour. The free 1-800 numbers
can only be accessed in North America.

Connecticut
1-800 282 6863

New Hampshire
1-800 258 3608

Maine
1-800 777 0317

Rhode Island
401 222 2601

Massachusetts
1-800 227 3608

Vermont
802 828 3239

Reporting to the guide

Please write and tell us about your experiences of small hotels, guest houses and inns, whether good or bad, whether listed in this edition or not. As well as hotels in New England, we are interested in hotels in Britain, France, Spain, Austria, Germany, Switzerland and Greece. We assume that reporters have no objections to our publishing their views unpaid.

Readers whose reports prove particularly helpful may be invited to join our Travellers' Panel. Members give us notice of their own travel plans; we suggest hotels that they might inspect, and help with the cost of accommodation.

The address to write to us is:

Editor, *Charming Small Hotel Guides*,
Duncan Petersen Publishing Limited,
31 Ceylon Road,
London W14 0PY.

Checklist

Please use a separate sheet of paper for each report; include your name, address and telephone number on each report.

Your reports will be received with particular pleasure if they are typed, and if they are organized under the following headings:

Name of establishment
Town or village it is in, or nearest
Full address, including postcode
Telephone number
Time and duration of visit
The building and setting
The public rooms
The bedrooms and bathrooms
Physical comfort (chairs, beds, heat, light, hot water)
Standards of maintenance and housekeeping
Atmosphere, welcome and service
Food
Value for money

We assume that in writing you have no objections to your views being published unpaid, either verbatim or in an edited version. Names of major outside contributors are acknowledged, at the editor's discretion, in the guide.

NEW YORK

NEW YORK CITY

BOX TREE

⤳ RESTAURANT-HOTEL ⤳

250 East 49th Street, New York, NY 10017
TEL (212) 7588320 **FAX** (212) 3083899
WEBSITE www.theboxtree.com

THE BOX TREE HAS LONG been a fixture of the New York restaurant scene; it joined the hotel listings in 1986. Its Midtown location is in a mixed neighbourhood of shops and residences, with brown-stones on the side streets and high rise buildings on the avenues. The entrance sets the style: gold-coloured leaves on metal 'vines' and the Box Tree name scripted on an intricate, European-style hanging sign.

The interior is intimate and rather precious: not the place for fans of pure lines and Scandinavian design. As in a collector's home, rooms are dense with eye-catching objects. In the reception room, dark green walls and a polished brick floor provide a backdrop for the Spanish campaign chest that serves as a message desk for guests. The cream and pastel staircase has Gaudi-esque swirls. Painted patterns on doors, such as the Monet-like water lily motif, make the corridors more interesting than most hotels. Bedrooms are plush, with individual decorative themes such as Egyptian, Chinese, or Japanese. Given the attention to detail everywhere else, bathrooms are surprisingly mundane. The price includes a credit toward dinner in the well-known restaurant.

⤳

NEARBY UN HQ, Rockefeller Center, St Patrick's Cathedral.
LOCATION between Second and Third Avenues; garage parking
FOOD breakfast, lunch, dinner
PRICE rooms $$$$ with breakfast and credit for dinner
ROOMS 13 double; all have bath or shower, air-conditioning, phone, TV, hairdrier, safe, fireplace **FACILITIES** reception area
SMOKING no
CREDIT CARDS AE, MC, V
CHILDREN welcome
DISABLED not suitable
CLOSED never
PROPRIETOR Gila Baruch

NEW YORK

NEW YORK CITY

CHELSEA HOTEL

~ HISTORIC HOTEL ~

222 West 23rd Street, New York, NY 10011
TEL (212) 2433700 **FAX** (212) 2433700
WEBSITE www.chelseahotel.com

WE DO NOT RECOMMEND THIS FOR EVERYONE. Built in 1882 as co-operative apartments, it's a landmark in the city, epitomising the Bohemian side of New York. The subject of three films, it was the inspiration for the 1960s song *Chelsea Morning*. The roll-call of writers in residence ranges from Mark Twain to Dylan Thomas; Arthur Miller penned *After the Fall* here, Arthur C Clarke wrote the screen-play for *2001: a Space Odyssey*. Numerous well-known artists and musicians have also checked in.

The entrance is full of paintings, sculpture and thirsty plants, creating a cluttered, casual, run-down look. Perhaps this is a deliberate ploy to discourage any bourgeois would-be guests. In fact, the bedrooms above are clean, neat and functional. The studio we saw had two double beds, a view of the Empire State Building, a small refrigerator and a stove. Cupboards were modern, blonde wood; the bathroom was 1930s vintage with black and blue tiles and a pedestal wash-basin.

Go elsewhere for elegance, deluxe service and five-star furnishings. People come here to wallow in the New York experience. The neighbourhood is young, artistic and lively.

~

NEARBY Greenwich Village, Penn Station, Madison Square Garden.
LOCATION mixed area between 7th and 8th Avenues; valet car parking
FOOD lunch, dinner
PRICE room only $$-$$$$
ROOMS 110; all have bath or shower, air-conditioning, phone, TV, safe
FACILITIES reception area, lift/elevator
SMOKING permitted
CREDIT CARDS AE, MC, V
CHILDREN welcome
DISABLED not suitable
CLOSED never
MANAGER Stanley Bard

NEW YORK

NEW YORK CITY

THE FRANKLIN

~ TOWNHOUSE ~

164 East 87th Street, New York, NY 10128
Tel (212) 3691000; (877) 847444 **Fax** (212) 3698000
E-MAIL franklin@boutiquehg.com **WEBSITE** www.franklinhotel.com

BETWEEN LEXINGTON AND THIRD Avenues on the Upper East Side, this is just a short walk from major museums plus auction houses, restaurants and expensive shops. There is a traditional look about the exterior of this hotel, with window boxes full of ivy and geraniums and a brass canopy shading the entrance. Inside, however, the style is modern and minimalist, reminiscent of art deco in the use of grey with black accents. Where most posh city hotels have elaborate arrangements of flowers, here a simple vase of red roses provides a statement of colour. Similarly, black and white photographs of neighbourhood scenes hang on walls. Overall, lighting is subdued.

There are only six bedrooms on each floor. These have canopy beds and cedar cupboards plus specially-designed furniture of black granite, cherry wood or steel. In smaller rooms the imaginative use of space and streamlined furnishings eliminate any feeling of being cramped. Bathrooms have reglazed cast-iron tubs. Well-priced, this attracts business clientele, including people working at nearby museums, and families at weekends. Guests may use a nearby health club at reduced rates.

~

NEARBY museums, Carl Schurz Park, East River.
LOCATION between Lexington and Third Avenue; free covered car parking
FOOD breakfast
PRICE rooms $$$$ with breakfast
ROOMS 24 double; 24 single; all have bath or shower, air-conditioning, phone, TV and VCR, radio, hairdrier
FACILITIES breakfast room, sitting room, lift/elevator
CREDIT CARDS AE, MC, V
SMOKING some rooms
CHILDREN welcome
DISABLED not suitable
CLOSED never
MANAGER Jeff Stegman

NEW YORK

NEW YORK CITY

THE LIBRARY HOTEL

~ CITY HOTEL ~

299 Madison Avenue, New York, NY 10017
TEL (212) 9834500 **FAX** (212) 4999099
E-MAIL reservations@libraryhotel.com **WEBSITE** www.libraryhotel.com

THESE DAYS, the term 'boutique hotel' is a cliché; nevertheless, it accurately describes this recently opened Midtown stopover. The name refers to the New York Public Library, only a block away and the library theme continues with floor-to-ceiling bookshelves in the reception area. Here, instead of pigeon-holes, card index drawers with Dewey system 'catalog' numbers instead of room numbers. Rooms are named after library subject categories – and have appropriate books. Our inspectors slept in 'European religion' no 12.06, in a comfortable, urban chic style.

At street level is a restaurant (buzzing non-resident trade), sitting area and computer room (free internet access). The top floor has a roof terrace, conservatory and 'Writers Room'. Passes to the New York Sports Clubs are complimentary. Guests include youngish business people and academic types. Despite all this and the young and friendly staff, there are drawbacks: nearby building work can start early in the morning; the self-service breakfast was disappointing; Venetian blinds in bedrooms offer only a partial blackout.

~

NEARBY Times Square, theatres, Macy's.
LOCATION at 41st Street; garage nearby
FOOD breakfast, lunch, dinner, snacks
PRICE rooms $$$$ with breakfast
ROOMS 60 double; all have air-conditioning, phone, TV, VCR, radio, data port, minibar, hairdrier, safe
FACILITIES restaurant, sitting room, lift/elevator; terrace
SMOKING some rooms
CREDIT CARDS AE, DC, MC, V
CHILDREN welcome
DISABLED 3 rooms
CLOSED never
MANAGER Craig Spitzer

NEW YORK

NEW YORK CITY

THE SHERRY-NETHERLAND

~ HISTORIC HOTEL ~

781 Fifth Avenue, New York, NY 10022-1046
TEL (212) 3552800; (800) 2474377 **FAX** (212) 3194306
WEBSITE www.sherrynetherland.com

THIS NEW YORK CLASSIC hardly seems a small hotel, towering above the Plaza in a great location where Fifth Avenue meets Central Park. However, staying there recently we thought again. Although there are 400 bedrooms, only a quarter are used for transient guest nights; the rest are private long-rental apartments. Once inside, it has the feel of a small – well, for New York, smallish hotel – with its intimate and amazingly decorated lobby, based on the Vatican library, and cosy restaurant. Other guests seem curiously scarce. Service is personal, discrete. Rooms are, for this city, cavernous; decoration is in restrained good taste, with beautifully mirrored bathrooms and many original features dating from the 1920s when ice cream magnate Louis Sherry created the hotel. It's the choice of heads of state and rock stars with nothing to prove and a taste for understated luxury, much less flash than Manhattan's grand hotels. We think that readers who appreciate an historic experience may well find – provided cost is not an issue – that this is a place with a special charm and character. Breakfast, video library and fitness centre are all within the room price.

~

NEARBY Central Park, Fifth Avenue shopping, museums.
FOOD Midtown at 59th Street; car parking by arrangement
PRICE rooms $$$$
ROOMS 120; all have bath or shower, air-conditioning, phone, TV, video, fax, radio, minibar, hairdrier
FACILITIES dining room, sitting room, fitness area, lift/elevator
SMOKING some rooms
CREDIT CARDS AE, DC, MC, V
CHILDREN welcome
DISABLED 6 adapted rooms
CLOSED never
MANAGER Louis Ventresca

CONNECTICUT

GRISWOLD INN
~ HISTORIC INN ~

36 Main Street, Essex, CT 06426
TEL (860) 7671776 FAX (860) 7670481
E-MAIL griswoldinn@snet.net WEBSITE www.griswoldinn.com

IN 1995, the Griswold Inn was bought by the Paul brothers, only the fifth time this hostelry has changed hands since it opened in 1776. The Pauls grew up in Essex, so they know 'the Gris' of old. They added to the fine collection of maritime art, which reflects the town's boat-building tradition. They kept distinctive features of the dining rooms: the river-scene mural in the Steamboat Room, which moves, imitating the motion of waves at the flick of a switch; the Covered Bridge room that is, or was, a real bridge, transported from New Hampshire; and the Gun Room's antique firearms dating back to the 15thC. They didn't dare change the Tap Room, a local haunt like an English pub. However, the Pauls did renovate the bedrooms, decorating them in soft Colonial tones of sage green and Wedgwood blue. In a separate building, there is a sitting-room with television and refrigerator for guests' use. Although the inn is bustling and commercial standards remain high.

Essex is a charming, historic town; on summer weekends, it is crowded with visitors touring the antiques and crafts shops and admiring the fine 18th-19thC homes. ~

NEARBY Connecticut River Museum; Gillette Castle; beaches.
LOCATION in village; car parking
FOOD breakfast, lunch, dinner
PRICE rooms $$-$$$ with breakfast
ROOMS 16 double; 15 suites; all have bath or shower, air-conditioning, phone, radio
FACILITIES 5 dining rooms, bar; garden
SMOKING no
CREDIT CARDS AE, MC, V
CHILDREN welcome
DISABLED not suitable
CLOSED restaurant only, Christmas Day
PROPRIETORS Paul brothers

CONNECTICUT

GREENWICH

THE HOMESTEAD

~ RESTAURANT INN ~

420 Field Point Road, Greenwich, CT 06830
TEL (203) 8697500 FAX (203) 8697502
WEBSITE www.homesteadinn.com

JUST INSIDE the Connecticut border, Fairfield County is one of the wealthiest in the USA, nicknamed the Gold Coast because of the magnates who commute to New York City from here. To be rated one of its top restaurants is a serious commendation. "Restaurant Thomas Henkelmann is where you go if you want to really impress someone," one businessman told us, "and it has an impressive wine list." German-born Henkelmann, the chef/owner, has worked in some of France's finest restaurants. Many society events are held here, from weddings to celebratory parties because "it is old and established and you can't go wrong."

Henkelmann bought the famous inn in 1997, and in 2001, his wife, Theresa redecorated it completely. Now the bedrooms are stylish, a far cry from the Granny-style fussiness of many New England inns. Outside, the attractive Victorian Gothic style remains with its distinctive Italianate cupola and wrap-around veranda. Located in Belle Haven, which juts out into Long Island Sound, this inn is an escape from New York City, with lawns, trees and a terrace with pink umbrellas in summer.

~

NEARBY museums, designer shops.
LOCATION in residential area, car parking
FOOD breakfast, lunch, dinner
PRICE rooms $$$-$$$$ with breakfast
ROOMS 19; all have bath or shower, air-conditioning, phone, TV, VCR, radio
FACILITIES 3 dining rooms, sitting room, bar; veranda, garden
SMOKING restricted
CREDIT CARDS AE, DC, MC, V
CHILDREN welcome
DISABLED 1 suite
CLOSED never
PROPRIETORS the Henkelmanns

CONNECTICUT

IVORYTON

COPPER BEECH
RESTAURANT INN

46 Main Street, Ivoryton, CT 06442
TEL (860) 7670330; (888) 8092056 FAX (860) 7677840
WEBSITE www.copperbeechinn.com

THE BRANCHES OF THE HUGE, old tree that gives this inn its name spread out across the main street of Ivoryton, itself named for the local industry. The manufacture of ivory piano keys, buttons and combs died out in the 1940s; now the village is better known for its summer theatre and this restaurant, which has the feel of a French *auberge*. Menus reflect the sophistication of the clientele, many of whom drive up from New York City for the weekend. "People come just for our *ris de veau*," Eldon Senner told our inspector, "but the bouillabaisse is another favourite." Autumn brings venison in hearty sauces but ice cream and sorbet are made year-round by chef Robert Celentano, who trained at the CIA and worked in France. Wines from Bordeaux are a speciality but California is also well-represented.

Although the first impression is rather gloomy, with lots of dark wood, the conservatory is bright and sunny. In the Carriage House, ramps provide wheelchair access to five of the bedrooms but all open on to wooden decks. Furnishings are in subdued tones of cream with pink or blue and there are plenty of four-poster and canopy beds.

NEARBY Goodspeed opera; scenic railway; coast.
LOCATION at east end of village; car parking
FOOD breakfast, Sunday lunch, dinner
PRICE rooms $$-$$$ with breakfast
ROOMS 13 double; all have bath or shower, air-conditioning; some haveTV, radio
FACILITIES 4 dining rooms, sitting room; garden
SMOKING restricted
CREDIT CARDS AE, DC, MC, V
CHILDREN over 10
DISABLED 5 rooms
CLOSED 1 week early Jan; restaurant only, Monday (and Tuesday Jan to Mar)
PROPRIETORS Eldon and Sally Senner

CONNECTICUT

MYSTIC

OLD MYSTIC INN

~ VILLAGE BED-AND-BREAKFAST ~

52 Main Street, Mystic, CT 06372
TEL (860) 5729422 FAX (860) 5729954
E-MAIL omysticinn@aol.com WEBSITE www.oldmysticinn.com

MYSTIC SEAPORT is a fascinating maritime museum, with historic ships plus working 'artisans' such as rope makers and printers. A short walk south is the old town of Mystic with its handsome 18th-19thC homes. Do not confuse this with Olde Mistick Village, a 'Colonial' complex of shops, just off Interstate 95.

In 1999, Michael Cardillo took over the inn, a 1784 home that became the Old Mystic Bookshop in the 20thC. Here, bedrooms show his attention to detail. Named after American authors, each comes with a synopsis of the writer's life and some of his or her works. There are quilts and chintzy fabrics, antiques and reproductions; nothing is out of place. The enthusiasm of Michael and his youthful team of helpers offsets an atmosphere that could be maiden-auntish. Rooms in the Carriage House are less atmospheric, but still pleasant and roomy, with sitting areas. The Keeping Room, the only public room, is a thoroughfare for getting to other parts of the building, so it is not for quiet reading or conversation. The breakfast room is charmingly wooden and creaky; the 'country breakfast', Michael's tour de force, is elaborate and plentiful. A new entry; reports welcome.

~

NEARBY Mystic Seaport, Mystic Aquarium; Stonington.
LOCATION in historic town centre; car parking
FOOD breakfast
PRICE rooms $$ with breakfast
ROOMS 8 double; all have bath or shower, air-conditioning, radio; 6 fireplaces
FACILITIES sitting room, breakfast room; garden
SMOKING no
CREDIT CARDS AE, MC, V
CHILDREN over 12 **DISABLED** not suitable
CLOSED never
PROPRIETOR Michael Cardillo

CONNECTICUT

MYSTIC

STEAMBOAT INN

~ RIVERSIDE INN ~

73 Steamboat Wharf, Mystic, CT 06355
TEL (860) 5368300 FAX (860) 5369528
E-MAIL sbwharf@aol.com WEBSITE www.visitmysic.com/steamboat

THE RIVERSIDE TOWN of Mystic is a special place for Americans, with its history of sailing ships and a living naval museum. A sleek schooner is anchored just outside this inn that is right on the water. Although there are water colours of lighthouses and ships by Carol Connor, the wife of one of the owners, the atmosphere is not overtly nautical.

All the bedrooms except one overlook the Mystic River; all are named after schooners with local connections; and all have whirlpool baths. Most have a fireplace. Plain colours predominate, perhaps with patterned bedspreads or curtains for contrast. Victoria is sage-green, Summer Girl has yellow walls. All are light, open and relaxing after a hard day's sightseeing. A continental style breakfast is served in the cheerful Common Room, which, unfortunately, overlooks the town parking lot. Many guests retreat with a tray to their rooms, all of which have a sitting area with a sofa and chair. In Kathleen, this can be closed off, providing a room for children. Some also have a microwave or a 'wet bar' (mini-fridge and sink). Summer traffic in Mystic is slow; leave your car, from here you can walk to all the attractions.

~

NEARBY Mystic Seaport, Aquarium; Coast Guard Academy.
LOCATION in town; public car parking
FOOD breakfast
PRICE rooms $$-$$$$ with breakfast
ROOMS 10 double; all have bath or shower, air-conditioning, phone, TV; some with minibar **FACILITIES** sitting room
SMOKING restricted
CREDIT CARDS AE, MC, V
CHILDREN over 12
DISABLED 4 rooms
CLOSED never
MANAGER Diana Stadtmiller

CONNECTICUT

NEW HAVEN

THREE CHIMNEYS INN

~ TOWN HOUSE HOTEL ~

1201 Chapel St, New Haven, CT 06511
TEL (203) 7891201; (800) 4431554 FAX (203) 7767363
E-MAIL chimney@aol.com WEBSITE www.threechimneysinn.com

THE HOME of ivy-clad Yale University, New Haven is short of charming small hotels, so this inn fills a need, appealing to parents of students and business travellers alike. Once a funeral parlour, there is nothing depressing now about the atmosphere; it looks and feels like a comfortable Victorian home, with a dining-room for breakfast and an old-fashioned drawing-room for afternoon tea. What was listed in the first edition of our guide as the Inn at Chapel West changed hands in 1995. This has resulted in a both a facelift and a change of name.

Two bedrooms are on the ground floor, the rest are up the dramatic three-storey, polished wood staircase. Each bedroom is totally different, with high-quality antique or reproduction furniture. Room 11 boasts a tin ceiling and a collection of ceramic plates, while Room 33 has a 'Grandma's Attic' feel with its small windows under the sloping roof. Standards are high, with fresh flowers and proper reading lamps by beds. Our inspector found 'an interesting book thoughtfully left on the bed'. Convenient for downtown New Haven, with its shops and inventive new restaurants nearby, such as the Roomba.

~

NEARBY Yale University; art galleries, theatre.
LOCATION in town; own car parking
FOOD breakfast
PRICE rooms $$$ with breakfast
ROOMS 10 double. all with bath or shower; all rooms have air-conditioning, phone, TV, VCR, radio, hairdrier
FACILITIES dining room, sitting room, conference room
SMOKING restrictedCREDIT CARDS AE, MC, V CHILDREN over 12
DISABLED 2 rooms CLOSED 1 week Christmas
INNKEEPER Michael Marra

CONNECTICUT

NORTH STONINGTON

ANTIQUES & ACCOMMODATIONS

VILLAGE BED-AND-BREAKFAST

32 Main Street, North Stonington, CT 06359
TEL (860) 5351736; (800) 5547829 FAX (860) 5352613
WEBSITE www.visitmystic.com/antiques

ANN AND THOMAS GRAY are antique dealers by profession; they decided to offer 'accommodations' after enjoying bed-and-breakfasts on buying trips in the West of England. Not surprisingly, the house is full of interesting furniture, such as the mahogany linen press that camouflages the television in the sitting room. In the dining room, unusual blue flower-sconces stand out against yellow wallpaper and the polished table reflects candle-light at breakfast, which is a four-course affair. Breads are home-made, herbs and flowers come straight from the garden, including 'Johnny jump-ups' (violets) that provide edible decoration.

In fine weather, guests eat on the small patio by the crab-apple tree. Plants are chosen for scent as well as colour and fresh bouquets are in bedrooms, some of which are full of patterns, others plainer, with hand-painted motifs on white walls toning with the pattern of the curtains.

The main house is for adults but 'children who appreciate antiques' are welcome, staying in the garden cottage, which has a modern kitchen plus three bedrooms. They have recently bought the 1840 farm house next door, with two more luxury rooms.

NEARBY Long Island Sound; Mystic seaport; Foxwoods casino.
LOCATION in village; car parking
FOOD breakfast
PRICE rooms $$-$$$ with breakfast
ROOMS 11 rooms; all have bath or shower, air-conditioning; some withTV, radio
FACILITIES dining room, sitting room; terrace, garden
SMOKING no
CREDIT CARDS MC, V
CHILDREN welcome
DISABLED not suitable
CLOSED never
PROPRIETORS Ann and Thomas Gray

CONNECTICUT

NORWALK

SILVERMINE TAVERN

~ COLONIAL TAVERN ~

194 Perry Avenue, Nowalk CT 06850
TEL (203) 8474558 FAX (203) 8479171
E-MAIL innkeeper@silverminetavern.com WEBSITE www.silverminetavern.com

THE MOST IMPORTANT thing to know about this 18thC tavern is how to find it. Without a map, you, like our inspector, could have an exasperating time driving around Norwalk. When he finally arrived, he found huge throngs enjoying Sunday brunch, but away from the boisterous dining rooms the inn was remarkably serene.

Frank Whiteman treads a narrow path between cultured history and brash folksiness. The dining rooms are pure Colonial, with the brick and bare-board look that tourists expect. Copper and iron pots hang from the ceiling, a tailor's dummy represents Miss Abigail 'once the only woman in Connecticut permitted by law to stand within three feet of a bar'. Food is traditional rather than gourmet: chowder, chicken pies, and honeybuns, the house speciality. By contrast, the parlour looks like an English country house with wing chairs, formal wallpaper and oil paintings. Much of the furniture is Queen Anne or Chippendale, thanks to John Byard, a 1920s owner who was an astute antiques dealer. Six pretty bedrooms are in the main house, five more above the country store across the street. With a rumbling waterfall and a mill pond, this is a pleasant, well-priced place to stay.

~

NEARBY Silvermine Guild of Art, South Norwalk Maritime Center.
LOCATION difficult to find; car parking
FOOD breakfast, lunch, dinner
PRICE rooms $$ with breakfast
ROOMS 11 double; all have bath or shower
FACILITIES 6 dining rooms, sitting room; terrace
SMOKING restricted
CREDIT CARDS AE, MC, V
CHILDREN welcome
DISABLED not suitable
CLOSED never; restaurant only, Tues
PROPRIETOR Frank Whitman

CONNECTICUT

BEE AND THISTLE

~ HISTORIC HOUSE ~

100 Lime Street, Old Lyme, CT 06371
TEL (860) 434 1667; (800) 622 4946 FAX (860) 434 3402
E-MAIL info@beeandthistleinn.com WEBSITE www.beeandthistleinn.com

IN 2000, after many successful years, the Nelson family handed over to Philip and Marie Abrahams. These new owners left behind their famous family pub in Virginia for the quieter reaches of Lieutenant River, a tributary of the Connecticut River. "We want to keep the atmosphere the same, but make some changes, too," the Culinary Institute of America-trained chef explains. So rooms have been redecorated in cooler, less floral patterns. "We want to be less froo-froo, more period accurate." So the furnishings are their choice, not a decorator's, and are comfortable rather than elegant. There are four-poster beds and family heirlooms instead of priceless antiques. Offering more privacy is the separate cottage with a full kitchen plus a private garden and wooden deck.

Locals as well as overnight guests book into the dining room and two side-porches, where the menu is 'new American' but the chef is British: Francis Brooke-Smith, who trained at the Ritz Hotel in London. "We installed a new range for him, and a broiler for lighter dishes." Outside, at the back, Philip has opened up views over the sunken garden and large lawn.

~

NEARBY Florence Griswold Museum; Long Island Sound.
LOCATION in historic district; car parking
FOOD breakfast, lunch, dinner
PRICE rooms $-$$$
ROOMS 11 double; 1 cottage; most have bath or shower, air-conditioning, phone; some radio; TV in cottage
FACILITIES 4 dining rooms, 2 sitting rooms; garden
SMOKING restricted
CREDIT CARDS AE, DC, MC, V
CHILDREN over 12
DISABLED not suitable
CLOSED 2 weeks Jan; restaurant only, Tues, Sun lunch
PROPRIETORS Abrahams family

CONNECTICUT

OLD LYME

OLD LYME INN
∼ RESTORED FARMHOUSE ∼

85 Lyme Street, Old Lyme, CT 06371
TEL (860) 434 2600 FAX (860) 434 5352
E-MAIL keith@oldlymeinn.com WEBSITE www.oldlymeinn.com

IF YOU HAVEN'T VISITED in a while, be prepared for a surprise. Keith and Candy Green took over in 2001 and have given the inn an update. Keith, an ex-Madison Avenue advertising executive, has thrown out all the Victoriana, with its fishing and hunting trophies. Instead, colours are fresh greens and yellows, setting off his wife's impressive floral arrangements. The three huge urns in the Winslow Dining Room and Lounge always have striking displays.

The Green's new approach is also reflected in the menus. A summer dish might be crab cakes with a fresh mango salsa, while cooler weather brings honey-glazed lamb shoulder slowly roasted for eight hours, and served on mashed potatoes. At the turn of the century, Old Lyme was an artists' colony, focused on the home of Florence Griswold, now a museum. The inn's walls are hung with bold paintings by contemporary American artists, on loan from the nearby Cooley Gallery. By contrast, the pretty bedrooms have not been touched. Number 7 is particularly attractive, with its canopy bed and doors opening into the garden. More reports, please, on this 'newcomer'.

∼

NEARBY Florence Griswold Museum; Foxwoods casino.
LOCATION just off I-95 at exit 70; car parking
FOOD breakfast, lunch, dinner
PRICE rooms $$-$$$ with breakfast
ROOMS 13 double; all have bath or shower, air-conditioning, phone, TV, radio
FACILITIES 2 dining rooms, 2 sitting rooms, function room; garden
SMOKING restricted
CREDIT CARDS AE, DC, MC, V
CHILDREN welcome
DISABLED not suitable
CLOSED never
PROPRIETORS Keith and Candy Green

CONNECTICUT

RIDGEFIELD

THE ELMS

～ COLONIAL INN ～

500 Main Street, Ridgefield, CT 06877
TEL (203) 4382541 FAX (203) 4382541
E-MAIL innkeeper@elmsinn.com WEBSITE www.elmsinn.com

RIDGEFIELD IS ONE of those refined, busy, small towns that is within reach of New York City folk escaping for weekends. The broad main street has antique shops and handsome houses, including this clapboard building that has been an inn since 1799, but was built even earlier by Amos Seymour in 1760. The Revolutionary Period is almost tangible with the beams and panelling inside, although the owner's wife, Susan Scala, has added a whimsical mural depicting historical events in the area.

Popular with locals, the main restaurant is leased to the enthusiastic team of Brendan and Cris Walsh, whose dishes are hearty, traditional and very American, with some engaging modern twists: Connecticut seafood stew, lobster shepherd's pie and apple pandowdy. In the Tavern, the pub food ranges from fresh ground burgers to smoked salmon sandwiches.

Of the bedrooms, we prefer those in the original inn, which have a Colonial atmosphere. The majority, however, are in the recently renovated annexe next door. Although attractive and comfortable, they have less character. All in all, this is a well-priced, useful base for exploring this part of Connecticut.

～

NEARBY Aldrich Museum of Contemporary Art, antiques shops.
LOCATION in town; car parking
FOOD breakfast, lunch, dinner
PRICE rooms $$ with breakfast
ROOMS 15 double; 5 suites; all have bath or shower, air-conditioning, phone, TV
FACILITIES 5 dining rooms, sitting room; terrace, garden
SMOKING restricted
CREDIT CARDS AE, DC, MC, V
CHILDREN welcome
DISABLED not suitable
CLOSED never
PROPRIETORS the Scala family

CONNECTICUT

SALISBURY

UNDER MOUNTAIN INN

~ BRITISH INN ~

482 Undermountain Road, Route 41, Salisbury, CT 06068
TEL (860) 4350242 FAX (860) 4352379
E-MAIL undermoutaininn@aol.com WEBSITE www.innbook.com

ANGLOPHILES THINK they have 'died and gone to heaven' in this rural valley on one of New England's prettiest stretches of country road. From the outside, this is just another carefully-restored 250-year old farmhouse in the Litchfield Hills, with requisite porch, maple trees and birches. A gigantic thorned locust tree, the oldest in the state, looms over the inn.

Once inside, however, the ambience is Old England rather than New. Peter Higginson, the innkeeper and chef, is British and worked his way round the world on passenger liners. His steak-and-kidney pie is well-made, the shepherd's pie and bangers and mash (sausages and mashed potatoes) use quality meats. The restaurant is not open to the public; dinner is part of the overnight experience.

Marged Higginson, an American who is as enthusiastic about local history as she is about Britain, organizes the steady supply of magazines and newspapers from Britain. Bedrooms are named after London landmarks: the smallest is Trafalgar Square; a large, upstairs corner room is Buckingham Gate, with a canopy bed and matching upholstery and wallpaper.

~

NEARBY Music Mountain, Sharon Playhouse, Tanglewood.
LOCATION on a country road; car parking
FOOD breakfast, dinner, snacks
PRICE DB&B from $$$
ROOMS 7 double; all have bath or shower
FACILITIES 3 dining rooms, 2 sitting rooms, pub; garden
SMOKING no
CREDIT CARDS MC, V
CHILDREN over 6
DISABLED not suitable
CLOSED never
PROPRIETORS Marged and Peter Higginson

CONNECTICUT

SALISBURY

WHITE HART

~ VILLAGE INN ~

The Village Green, Salisbury CT 06068
TEL (860) 435 0030; (800) 832 0041 FAX (860) 435 0040
E-MAIL innkeeper@whitehartinn.com WEBSITE www.whitehartinn.com

BURIED IN THE LITCHFIELD HILLS, Salisbury is a classic New England village, popular with weekenders from New York City. Scott Bok is the new owner of this 19thC-country inn that has long been a benchmark for excellence in the area. Scott took over from Terry and Juliet Moore back in 1998, but readers tell us that the changes have been minimal. In the Riga Room, formerly the American Grill, chef Brian Ruffner serves Modern American dishes, such as nut-crusted rack of lamb with a blackcurrant sauce. The familiar paintings of fruit and vegetables by Janet Rickus, who has a local studio, still line the walls. Breakfast, lunch and less formal evening meals are served in the Garden Room and Tap Room, with its two fireplaces, pub food and sports on the television. The chessboard in the panelled Hunt Room is a clue that this is a spot to relax.

Outside, the broad porch has pink wicker furniture; in the entrance, pale peach striped walls create a chic, sophisticated, yet cheerful look. The bedrooms are as stylish as ever, with pretty chintz fabrics, air-conditioning and practical bathrooms. More reports, please.

~

NEARBY antiques, Lime Rock Park car racing, golf, hiking.
LOCATION in village; car parking
FOOD breakfast, lunch, dinner
PRICE rooms $-$$$, breakfast extra
ROOMS 26 double; all have bath or shower, air-conditioning, phone, TV
FACILITIES 3 dining rooms, 2 sitting rooms, bar; porch
SMOKING restricted
CREDIT CARDS AE, DC, MC, V
CHILDREN welcome
DISABLED 1 room
CLOSED restaurant only, Sun toThurs
PROPRIETOR Scott Bok

CONNECTICUT

SOUTH WOODSTOCK

INN AT WOODSTOCK HILL

~ COUNTRY INN ~

Route 169, PO Box 98, 94 Plaine Hill Road, South Woodstock, CT 06267
TEL (860) 9280528 FAX (860) 9283236
E-MAIL innwood@snet.net WEBSITE www.webtravels.com/woodstockhill

NORTH-EASTERN CONNECTICUT is an area of gently rolling hills and fields. This 'quiet corner' of the state rewards exploration, particularly by bicycle, since the back roads are virtually empty of traffic. For nearly 180 years, this farmhouse has dominated the landscape, its hilltop setting looking west across meadows to woods and east over a wide valley.

This is not the sort of inn that tries to take you back in time, or strives for the 'private home' atmosphere. Forget the lace fripperies, the patchwork quilts and personal photographs. This is a country hotel that caters to couples and to executive meetings, to individual diners and to weddings. Richard Naumann, from Frankfurt, is the chef and innkeeper. The low-ceilinged dining room, with its warm peachy red decoration, is probably prettier by candle light than daylight.

Overall, the quality of the furnishings is high, with pretty fabrics and thick carpets. In the bedrooms, you may find a cathedral ceiling, a four-poster bed or a fireplace, but all have telephones and televisions. The guest cottage is ideal for friends or a small family reunion. The three bedrooms each have separate bathrooms, but there is a shared sitting room.

~

NEARBY hiking, cycling.
LOCATION on 'Scenic Route 169'; car parking
FOOD breakfast, lunch, dinner
PRICE rooms $-$$ with breakfast
ROOMS 22 double; all have bath or shower, air-conditioning, phone, TV, radio
FACILITIES 2 dining rooms, 4 sitting rooms, bar; terrace, garden
SMOKING restricted
CREDIT CARDS MC, V
CHILDREN welcome
DISABLED 1 room
CLOSED restaurant only, Sun night, Mon lunch
PROPRIETOR Richard Naumann

CONNECTICUT

LORD THOMPSON MANOR

~ COUNTRY MANSION ~

Route 200, PO Box 428, Thompson, CT 06277
TEL (860) 9233886 FAX (860) 9239310
E-MAIL mail@lordthompsonmanor.com WEBSITE www.lordthompsonmanor.com

FROM ROUTE 200, the long, bumpy drive leads through woods to a plain-looking house with a putty-coloured, stucco exterior. This nondescript outside belies the luxury inside this 30-room manor. Jackie and Andrew Silverston brought it in 1989 and her career as a designer/decorator shows in the stylish furnishings. She is also keen on horses, so bedrooms are named for various breeds: Palomino, Morgan and Arabian. Thoroughbred I is pine green and burgundy, with an oriental carpet for extra colour.

The sitting room looks welcoming despite the formality of the high ceilings, wood-panelling and parquet floors. French windows lead on to the patio, which looks over lawns to the fields and rolling hills that are part of this large estate. With additional sitting rooms plus a dining room, there are more communal areas than in many bed-and-breakfast inns and it is often taken over for weddings, family reunions and executive meetings. A full breakfast is served and dinner can be arranged. They will even prepare a candle-lit bubble bath for guests: quite a change from the days when this provided living quarters for the priests who taught at the nearby Roman Catholic school.

~

NEARBY antique shops in Putnam.
LOCATION between I-395 and village of Thompson; car parking
FOOD breakfast
PRICE rooms $$ with breakfast
ROOMS 2 double; 4 suites; all have bath or shower
FACILITIES dining room, 3 sitting rooms; terrace, garden
SMOKING restricted
CREDIT CARDS MC, V
CHILDREN not suitable
DISABLED not suitable
CLOSED never
PROPRIETORS Jackie and Andrew Silverston

CONNECTICUT

WASHINGTON

MAYFLOWER

~ LUXURY RETREAT ~

Route 47, Washington, CT 06793
TEL (860) 8689466 FAX (860) 8681497
E-MAIL inn@mayflowerinn.com WEBSITE www.relaischateaux.fr/mayflower

SOME POSH HOTELS are opulent, as if to flaunt the vast sums spent on furnishings. This is more subdued, though 'not a detail has been overlooked nor a dollar unspent.' The clientele are city-types, escaping to the countryside but not to the simple life. Don't expect to make friends with the innkeeper; this has a professional, trained staff.

So what do you get for the (expensive) prices? Start with Limoges china in the dining rooms, where the sophisticated, modern-American cuisine ranges from lobster soup with Armagnac to roast wild striped bass. They smoke their own salmon and game sausage, make pasta and breads, and use organic produce. Wines are pricey. In the main house are also the parlour, the piano bar, and the wood-panelled, club-like library with plenty of books, some leather-bound. Throughout are antiques, Tabriz carpets and interior decorator colour schemes. The bedrooms and suites are in this and two other buildings; bathrooms are marble.

The fitness club has equipment plus exercise and yoga classes. Outside are impressive gardens, a tennis court and heated swimming pool.

~

NEARBY golf, hiking; antique shops; shooting school; Litchfield.
LOCATION on estate; car parking
FOOD breakfast, lunch, dinner
PRICE rooms $$$$
ROOMS 17 double; 8 suites; all have bath or shower, air-conditioning, phone, TV
FACILITIES 3 dining rooms, 3 sitting rooms, fitness club; garden, swimming pool
SMOKING restricted
CREDIT CARDS AE, MC, V
CHILDREN over 12
DISABLED not suitable
CLOSED never
MANAGER John Trevenen

RHODE ISLAND

BLOCK ISLAND

HOTEL MANISSES AND 1661 INN

～ VICTORIAN HOTELS ～

PO Box 1, 1 Spring Street, Block Island, RI 02807
TEL (401) 4662421; (800) 6264773 FAX (401) 4663162
E-MAIL biresorts@riconnect.com WEBSITE www.blockisland.com/biresorts

BLOCK ISLAND has only 800 permanent residents, but in summer this can swell to over 10,000 people, so car ferry and hotel reservations are essential on weekends. This is not a posh resort island; vacationers enjoy the beaches and spend time hiking, cycling, bird watching and, of course, fishing and boating in the Atlantic Ocean. Islanders since 1969, the Abrams family own the two main hotels along with four cottages.

Manisses is a Narrangansett Indian word meaning 'Island of the Little God'. This hotel has a Victorian look, mixing antiques and floral wallpaper with wicker furniture in rooms named for shipwrecks. Eat excellent fish in the sophisticated Dining Room, or relax in the more informal Gatsby Room or Upstairs Parlor. The 1661 Inn has a plainer, New England feel, with the rooms named for early settlers on the island. In summer, the breakfast buffet, with hot and cold dishes, is laid out in the dining room, which, along with the deck, looks straight out to the Atlantic Ocean. During the winter months, guests from both inns breakfast at the Manisses. They also have free tours of the island and, on Thursdays, watch the sunset at the North Lighthouse.

～

NEARBY ferry, water-sports, bicycle rental, lighthouses.
LOCATION near ferry landing; car parking
FOOD breakfast, dinner
PRICE rooms $-$$$$ with breakfast
ROOMS 39 in 2 inns; all have bath or shower, phone, radio
FACILITIES dining room, sitting room, bar; terrace, garden
SMOKING restricted
CREDIT CARDS AE, MC, V
CHILDREN welcome
DISABLED not suitable
CLOSED never
PROPRIETORS Abrams family

RHODE ISLAND

NEWPORT

ADELE TURNER INN

~ HISTORIC INN ~

93 Pelham Street, Newport 02840
TEL (401) 8471811; (800) 8451811 FAX (401) 8485850
E-MAIL innkeeper@adeleturnerinn.com WEBSITE www.adeleturnerinn.com

NEWPORT IS FAMOUS FOR its 'cottages', the summer homes built around the turn of the century by wealthy families such as the Vanderbilts. There is also the Jazz Festival in mid-July. Around the harbour, every other building seems to be on the National Historic Register, though Thames Street ('th-aymes') has its share of touristy T-shirt shops. This 1855 building, standing up the hill from the harbour, was formely the Admiral Benbow Inn. After Win Baker bought it in 2000, he completely renovated the place, putting in fine antiques, four poster bed and plush furnishings, then re-opened it as the Adele Turner Inn. Unusual features include 27 tall, arched windows. Room 11, Harborview Spa, has a private deck with hot tub and a panoramic view over the harbour. Start the day with morning coffee brought to your bedroom, followed by a full breakfast. Walk to all Newport's sights, then return in the afternoon to a tea table laden with tempting cakes. As for the name, Adele Turner was the mother of artist Beatrice Turner, whose works – originals and laser reproductions – feature here and in the Cliffside Inn (see page 58), also owned by Win Baker, nearby.

~

NEARBY historic mansions, harbour, sailing, beaches.
LOCATION in town; car parking
FOOD breakfast, afternoon tea
PRICE rooms $$-$$$$ with breakfast
ROOMS 10 double; 3 suites; all have bath or shower, air-conditioning, phone, TV, VCR, radio, hairdrier
FACILITIES sitting room/breakfast room, porch
SMOKING no
CREDIT CARDS AE, MC, V
CHILDREN over 13
DISABLED not suitable
CLOSED never
MANAGER Stephan Nicholas

RHODE ISLAND

NEWPORT

ADMIRAL FITZROY

~ HISTORIC BED-AND-BREAKFAST ~

398 Thames Street, Newport, RI 02840
TEL (401) 8488000; (866) 8488780 FAX (401) 8488006
E-MAIL info@admiralfitzroy.com WEBSITE www.admiralfitzroy.com

THIS BRICK INN stands amidst the hustle and bustle of Thames Street, with its restaurants and shops. Built as a convent in 1854 and moved from its original site, it was formerly one of several Newport inns owned by the Berriman family. There are new owners as of 2001, so we welcome reports.

Newport is – and always has been – one of the great sailing ports of the world. Not surprisingly, there is a strong nautical theme here in the inn. Admiral Fitzroy was the captain of HMS Beagle, the ship in which Charles Darwin sailed to the South Pacific and a portrait of the Admiral's wife still surveys the breakfast-room, where Jane Berriman's hand-painted bouquets and garlands decorate mint-green walls. Breakfast specialities include the imaginative 'pizza', a pancake served with lemon butter and surrounded by sautéed seasonal berries. Some bedrooms are decorated in pale colours with more Berriman painted flowers; others are more sombre, with dark furniture. Two of the most-requested rooms are at the top of the building, with decks and harbour views. The inn is a popular spot for weddings at weekends, so be sure to book well in advance.

~

NEARBY beaches, sailing; harbour, historic houses.
LOCATION near waterfront; car parking
FOOD breakfast
PRICE rooms $-$$$
ROOMS 18; all have bath or shower, air-conditioning, phone, TV, minibar, hairdrier
FACILITIES dining room, sitting room, lift/elevator; terrace, garden
SMOKING no
CREDIT CARDS AE, DC, MC, V
CHILDREN over 12
DISABLED 1 room
CLOSED never
INNKEEPER Heather Reeves

RHODE ISLAND

NEWPORT

CASTLE HILL INN & RESORT

BAY VIEW HOTEL

Ocean Drive, Newport, RI 02840
TEL (401) 8493800 FAX (401) 8493838
E-MAIL info@castlehillinn.com WEBSITE www.castlehillinn.com

AWAY FROM THE MIDDLE of Newport, Castle Hill is off Ocean Drive. It stands on a hill, surrounded by 40 acres, and has panoramic water views. This is where the Atlantic Ocean meets Narrangansett Bay; look across to Connecticut Island, up the bay to Newport Bridge. There is nothing undiscovered about this inn, but it changed dramatically in 1995. The 25 bedrooms were refurbished, and now have fireplaces, Jacuzzis, king size beds, and oriental rugs. The result is a more exclusive hotel; so make reservations well in advance for the famous circular Sunset Room with the gourmet-standard dinners. At breakfast, swimwear and sportswear are discouraged, and in the evenings, jackets are required. Yet well-behaved children are still welcome, and love the eight rooms in the Beach House, one of the few places in New England where you can step out of bed, on to the teak deck, and straight on to the white sands of a private beach. For atmosphere, however, nothing beats the Victorian feel of the nine bedrooms in the main mansion, built back in 1874, where floors still gently creak. Afternoon tea is based on the style of the best London hotels.

NEARBY beaches, historic houses; sailing; Newport harbour.
LOCATION overlooking water; car parking
FOOD breakfast, lunch, dinner
PRICE rooms $$$-$$$$ with breakfast
ROOMS 25; all have bath or shower, Jacuzzi
FACILITIES 3 dining rooms, bar; terrace, garden, beach
SMOKING restricted
CREDIT CARDS AE, MC, V
CHILDREN over 12
DISABLED not suitable
CLOSED never
MANAGER Chuck Flanders

RHODE ISLAND

CLIFFSIDE INN
~ VICTORIAN MANSION ~

2 Seaview Avenue, Newport, RI 02840
TEL (401) 8471811; (800) 8451811 FAX (401) 8485850
E-MAIL cliff@wsi.com WEBSITE www.cliffsideinn.com

FORMER OWNER Beatrice Turner is everywhere in this house: her self-portraits stare down from the staircase, sitting room and bedroom walls. Although her father forbade her to paint, she continued her obsession and when she died in 1948 the rooms overflowed with her work. Many of her paintings were then destroyed, so these are mainly laser reproductions.

The house was built in 1880 and the aim to recreate that period, with ornate beds, swathes of curtains and armoires. Bathrooms are some of the most luxurious we have seen anywhere. In the Governor's Suite, for example, the Victorian-style brass shower sprays water from four brass pipes, and there is also a modern whirlpool bathtub. Other bed and bathrooms are smaller but all have working fireplaces and stylish, expensive furnishings. Since 1995, the suites in Seaview Cottage, a low, separate building a few steps away in the garden, have catered for guests who want extra privacy. In the late afternoon, guests help themselves to afternoon tea in the sitting-room; a full breakfast, featuring crêpes with fresh strawberries or eggs Benedict, is served here in the morning.

~

NEARBY beaches, sailing; harbour, mansions.
LOCATION in residential area; car parking
FOOD breakfast, tea
PRICE rooms $$$-$$$$ with breakfast, tea
ROOMS 8 double; 5 suites; all have bath or shower, air-conditioning, phone, TV, VCR, radio; some, minibar
FACILITIES dining room/sitting room; porch, garden
SMOKING no CREDIT CARDS AE, MC, V
CHILDREN over 13
DISABLED not suitable
CLOSED never
MANAGER Stephan Nicholas

RHODE ISLAND

NEWPORT

ELM TREE COTTAGE

~ VICTORIAN MANSION ~

336 Gibbs Avenue, Newport, RI 02840
TEL (401) 8491610; (888) ELMTREE FAX (401) 8492084
E-MAIL t-p@elmtreebnb.com WEBSITE www.elm-tree.com

TALL, WEEPING BEECH TREES shade the entrance to this imposing summer home. Built in 1882 by New England architect William Ralph Emerson, the interior is more roomy than many bed-and-breakfasts. Five windows in the sitting room look out over the terraced garden and there is enough space for a baby grand piano plus sofas and armchairs. The Morning Room, with wicker furniture, was "where the lady of the house would meet with servants and plan the day," Thomas Malone told us. His wife, Priscilla, designed the stained-glass window panels that, with their antique and reproduction furniture, plus their collection of dolls, creates an eclectic look.

The Windsor Suite is feminine and heavily-decorated, its king-sized bed draped with fabric and piled with pillows. More sober is the Library, with 'hunting, shooting and fishing' prints and shelves with old books. The best bathroom is in the Harriman Room: a big shower and separate 'soaking tub' with a cushion to lie back on. Breakfast is a buffet but not a communal meal, since there are individual tables. The refrigerator in the bar is for guests' use. Verdict: posh furnishings, down-to-earth hosts.

~

NEARBY beaches, sailing; Newport harbour; historic houses.
LOCATION in residential area; car parking
FOOD breakfast
PRICE rooms $$$-$$$$
ROOMS 5 doubles, 1 suite; all have bath or shower, air-conditioning, radio; some have TV
FACILITIES dining room, 2 sitting rooms, bar; terrace, garden
SMOKING no
CREDIT CARDS AE, MC, V
CHILDREN over 14
DISABLED not suitable
CLOSED never
PROPRIETORS Priscilla and Tom Malone

RHODE ISLAND

NEWPORT

FRANCIS MALBONE HOUSE

~ COLONIAL BED-AND-BREAKFAST ~

392 Thames Street, Newport, RI 02840
TEL (401) 8460392; (800) 8460392 FAX (401) 8485956
E-MAIL innkeeper@malbone.com WEBSITE www.malbone.com

WHEN SHIPPING MERCHANT Francis Malbone built this mansion in 1760, it had a stately view of the harbour. Now Thames Street is lined with shops and restaurants. Yet because it stands back from the street, the atmosphere inside is surprisingly quiet. The look is uncluttered 'formal Colonial', with traditional furniture and colour combinations, such as restful burgundy and grey, pumpkin and white or slate-blue and cream.

Breakfast is come-when-you want from 8.30-10 am, perhaps with eggs benedict or waffles plus the usual fresh fruit, cereals and pastries. The huge fireplace in the dining room is a reminder that this was once the kitchen. Behind a door is the servants' staircase that goes all the way up to the attic. In the hall, a trapdoor led to a tunnel down to the wharf, a route supposedly used for smuggling rum. Some bedrooms have fireplaces; all have four-poster beds and white linens embroidered with 'M'. Views are to the water or over the peaceful garden behind, with its 300-year old maple. The inn has grown in the past five years, with nine new rooms, plus two suites in the 250 year-old Benjamin Moore House. These maintain the same high standards of both taste and comfort.

~

NEARBY beaches, sailing; Newport harbour; historic houses.
LOCATION near Newport Harbour; car parking
FOOD breakfast
PRICE rooms $$-$$$ with breakfast
ROOMS 20; all have bath or shower, air-conditioning
FACILITIES dining room, sitting room; terrace, garden
SMOKING no
CREDIT CARDS AE, MC, V
CHILDREN over 14
DISABLED not suitable
CLOSED 6 Jan to May (except weekends)
MANAGER Will Dewey

RHODE ISLAND

PROVIDENCE

THE OLD COURT

~ HISTORIC BED-AND-BREAKFAST ~

144 Benefit Street, Providence, RI 02903
TEL (401) 7512002 FAX (401) 2726566
E-MAIL reserve@oldcourt.com WEBSITE www.oldcourt.com

PROVIDENCE IS AN OVERLOOKED GEM of a city, founded in 1636 and with a host of historic houses. It is no theme park, however: the Colonial, Federal and Victorian buildings are homes, museums and, in this case, a bed-and-breakfast. The Old Court is on Benefit Street, known as the 'Mile of History', where the brick houses with iron boot scrapers could have been transported from Old England. Built in 1863, this plain building was bought in 1986 by John Rosenblatt, a former professor. Having renovated the stairs, floors and fire-places, he added antiques and reproduction furniture. Comfortable but not plush, the style is Victorian but without excessive drapery or heavy patterns.

The original kitchen is the small Stove Room, with a black antique stove and brass bed. Upstairs, the Chippendale Room is particularly large, with champagne-coloured wallpaper, a carved bed and generous bathroom. Some rooms at the back have views of the state capitol building, whose dome is floodlit at night. Many guests are parents of students at nearby colleges. A continental breakfast is served in the dining room, which has a lived-in look and doubles as a sitting room.

~

NEARBY historic sights, museums, colleges.
LOCATION in historic district; car parking
FOOD breakfast
PRICE rooms $$ with breakfast
ROOMS 10 double; 1 suite; all have bath or shower, air-conditioning, phone; some with TV, minibar
FACILITIES dining room/sitting room
SMOKING permitted CREDIT CARDS AE, MC, V
CHILDREN over 12
DISABLED not suitable
CLOSED never
PROPRIETOR John Rosenblatt

MASSACHUSETTS

BOSTON

XV BEACON
～ LUXURY HOTEL ～

15 Beacon St, Boston, MA 02108
TEL (617) 6701500; (877) xvbeacon FAX (617) 6702525
E-MAIL hotel@xvbeacon.com WEBSITE www.xvbeacon.com

"TOTAL LUXURY" reads the report on this hotel that opened in 1999. Find it just a few steps from the State House, in the heart of downtown. No money was spared in transforming what was a 1903 Beaux Arts office building into an hotel. Although the ornate façade was retained, along with the original cage elevator, the look throughout is contemporary, masculine and rather sombre: chocolate brown and taupe colour schemes, dark mahogany panelling and white marble floors. It all adds up to an atmosphere that is subdued, calm and very expensive.

Although couples and families are welcome, XV Beacon is designed to cater to the business executive's every need. Each of the spacious bedrooms has fast internet access, a colour fax/printer/copier and private telephone and fax numbers. Our reporter also noted the top quality mattresses and linens, and the windows that actually opened. Then, there are the personalized business cards and use of the hotel's chauffeured car. The restaurant, The Federalist, has a well-thought out modern-American menu and an outstanding wine collection of 17,000 bottles, including fine and rare vintages.

NEARBY Freedom Trail sights, State House, Beacon Hill.
LOCATION downtown Boston; valet parking
FOOD breakfast, lunch, dinner
PRICE rooms $$$$
ROOMS 61; all have bath or shower, air-conditioning, phone, fax, TV, CDs, radio, minibar, hairdrier, safe
FACILITIES sitting area, restaurant, fitness area, lift/elevator; terrace, nearby health clubSMOKING some rooms
CREDIT CARDS AE, DC, MC, V CHILDREN welcome
DISABLED 3 rooms
CLOSED never
MANAGER William J Sander III

MASSACHUSETTS

BOSTON

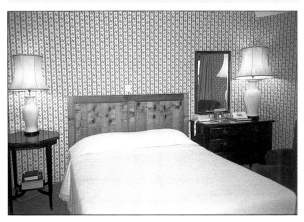

BEACON HILL HOTEL & BISTRO

~ BOUTIQUE HOTEL ~

25 Charles St, Boston, MA 02114
TEL (617) 7237575; (888) 959 BHHB FAX (617) 7237525
E-MAIL stay@beaconhillhotel.com WEBSITE www.beaconhillhotel.com

ANOTHER WELCOME addition to the Boston hotel scene, this establishment opened at the end of 2000. In Europe, small city hotels with restaurants are common; in the United States, they are a rarity. Here, two 19thC-townhouses have been converted to provide 13 bedrooms, named for members of the owners' families. The rooms are undeniably small, so those accustomed to spacious surroundings may feel cramped. However, we liked the cool colours, the louvred shutters, the trendy flat television monitors and the dramatic black and white photographs. Besides, with so much to see and do in Boston, how much time would anyone spend in a hotel room?

With large windows, the street-level bistro looks and feels very French. Regulars come for breakfast, lunch and dinner and include residents of the posh 19thC townhouses on Beacon Hill, as well as those who work in the antiques shops and small businesses along Charles Street. Breakfast is included in the room price and guests may select anything from the menu; lunch and dinner choices range from bistro classics to modern dishes. There is a sitting area and a small roof terrace for guests.

~

NEARBY museums, Freedom Trail sights, Newbury Street shops.
LOCATION downtown; garage nearby
FOOD breakfast, lunch, dinner
PRICE rooms $$$-$$$$ with breakfast
ROOMS 12 double; 1 suites; all have bath or shower, air-conditioning, phone, TV, radio, hairdrier
FACILITIES restaurant, sitting area, lift/elevator; terrace
SMOKING no
CREDIT CARDS AE, DC, MC, V
CHILDREN welcome
DISABLED 1 room
CLOSED never
PROPRIETORS Cecilia and Peter Rait

MASSACHUSETTS

BOSTON

COPLEY INN
~ CITY HOTEL ~

19 Garrison Street, Boston, MA 02116
TEL (617) 2360300; (800) 2320306 FAX (617) 5360816
E-MAIL info@copleyinn.com WEBSITE www.copleyinn.com

THERE ARE THOUSANDS of bedrooms in the huge hotels that are in and around Copley Place. Down a side street of Huntington Avenue is the Copley Inn, which has 21. It does not try to compete with the facilities offered by its neighbours; it has no private parking, no lift/elevator and no food service. What this four-storey, century-old brownstone provides is, literally, a 'home from home'.

Each bedroom has a television and telephone, a dining-table and chairs plus a mini-kitchen. Furnishings are 'hotel' rather than 'inn', comfortable rather than luxurious: reproduction furniture, plain walls, patterned bedspreads and white venetian blinds. Bathrooms are modern; some only have showers. Number 302 has a small stained-glass window and a vine growing over the window looking down into St Botulph Street.

This is different from other hotels in this guide; we recommend it for convenience and price. The tourist trolley and T-stop are just a few minutes away, as are restaurants and cinemas. Rates for a week or more are particularly attractive. Families are welcome; children under 12 are free.

~

NEARBY Museum of Fine Arts, Symphony Hall, Back Bay shops, MBTA: Copley or Symphony Stations.
LOCATION off Huntington Avenue; parking on street
FOOD none
PRICE rooms $$
ROOMS 21 double; all have bath or shower, air-conditioning, phone, TV, radio, kitchenette
FACILITIES reception area
SMOKING no
CREDIT CARDS AE, MC, V
CHILDREN welcome
DISABLED not suitable
CLOSED never
MANAGER Sheila Losordo

MASSACHUSETTS

BOSTON

NEWBURY GUEST HOUSE

~ TOWN HOUSE BED-AND-BREAKFAST ~

261 Newbury Street, Boston, MA 02116
TEL (617) 4377666; (800) 4377666 FAX (617) 2624243
E-MAIL nghdesk@aol.com WEBSITE hagopianhotels.com

IN THE UNITED STATES, a 'guest-house' usually refers to simple accommodation; this is an exception. It is also an exception to our 25-room limit. Although this bed-and-breakfast inn expanded to 32 rooms in 1994, the ambience is still 'small' and the charm remains. Moreover, it is right on Newbury Street, among trendy shops, art galleries and restaurants. The Charles River and the Prudential Center are each five-minutes' walk away; Boston Common is five blocks downtown.

Nubar Hagopian was inspired to open a hotel when he visited France in 1984 and stayed in *auberges*; he had already renovated several brownstones in Boston and he and his son, Mark, designed these interiors themselves. Bedrooms have traditional furniture and patterned bedspreads. Prints on the walls are of famous paintings in the nearby Museum of Fine Arts. Although the standard of furnishings is high, they are not luxurious; prices, therefore, are attractive. One guest with a bad back was so impressed by the bed, he wanted to buy one like it. There is also a sofa-bed in most rooms; those at the back are quieter; local phone calls are free; a small patio faces the street. See also Harborside Inn (page 183).

~

NEARBY Charles River, historic sights, Cambridge.
LOCATION between Fairfield St and Gloucester St; car parking, small charge
FOOD breakfast
PRICE rooms $$ with breakfast
ROOMS 32 double; all have bath or shower, air-conditioning, phone, TV, radio
FACILITIES sitting room, lift/elevator; terrace
SMOKING permitted
CREDIT CARDS AE, DC, MC, V
CHILDREN welcome
DISABLED 2 rooms
CLOSED never
PROPRIETORS the Hagopian family

MASSACHUSETTS

BREWSTER

CAPTAIN FREEMAN INN
~ SEA-CAPTAIN'S HOME ~

15 Breakwater Road, Brewster, MA 02631
TEL (508) 8967481; (800) 8434664 FAX (508) 8965618
E-MAIL visitus@capecod.net WEBSITE www.captainfreemaninn.com

BREWSTER IS JUST ONE of the towns along Route 6A, the old Cape Cod highway, now lined with antique shops and craft galleries. It used to be known for its sea captains. This mansion was built in the 1860s by Captain Freeman, who brought the mahogany for the floors back from his voyages. An inn for over 50 years, Carol Edmondson has been here since 1991.

She inherited her passion for food from her Austrian grandmother, a professional chef. Cookbooks with her recipes for breakfast specialities such as butter rum baked apples and lemon muffins are for sale. Carol is a perfectionist: "I bring a suitcase, unpack and stay overnight to make sure the quilt smells fresh and the bedside light is good for reading." This is a stylish but informal inn; the large garden has croquet, badminton, and a swimming pool. Smokers beware: here, the ban on nicotine extends even to the porch. In winter, weekends are busy. Some guests walk the beach, others slump with a glass of hot mulled cider. Tom also runs innkeeping seminars, while Carol's cookery school, with dinner and wine tasting, is booked up well in advance.

~

NEARBY beaches, nature trails, cycling; antique shops.
LOCATION in village; car parking
FOOD breakfast
PRICE rooms $$-$$$ with breakfast
ROOMS 12; all have bath or shower, radio, air-conditioning, phone, TV
FACILITIES dining room, sitting room; garden, swimming pool
SMOKING no
CREDIT CARDS AE, MC, V
CHILDREN over 10
DISABLED not suitable
CLOSED never
PROPRIETORS the Edmondsons

MASSACHUSETTS

CAMBRIDGE

A CAMBRIDGE HOUSE

~ LUXURY BED-AND-BREAKFAST ~

2218 Massachusetts Avenue, Cambridge, MA 02140
TEL (617) 4916300; (800) 2329989 FAX (617) 8682848
E-MAIL innach@attibi.com WEBSITE www.acambridgehouse.com

ON A BUSY MAIN STREET in an undistinguished area, this plush bed-and-breakfast is popular with academics visiting nearby Harvard University. The yellow-painted outside is pretty enough, with a porch supporting a terrace above. The inside is a riot of decoration, swathed with fabrics and dense with pattern. Supposedly Victorian, this is more like an interior decorator's fantasy. Large bulls-eye mirrors and Chinese pottery, brassware and Japanese prints abound. Recorded chamber music is ever-present, as is a tray of tea, coffee and cookies (morning) or wine and cheese (afternoon).

In the main house, bedroom furnishings are piled layer upon layer: ruffles around the four-poster beds, canopies overhead and lacy bolsters on floral pillows. Most rooms have working fire places. Bathrooms vary in size but have modern fixtures. In the adjacent Carriage House, the four bedrooms are just as luxurious. Breakfasts are equally complex with strawberries and cream waffles or Italian sausages and breads. It would all have been too much for Boston's Puritan forefathers.

~

NEARBY Harvard University; Boston; MBTA: Davis Square, Porter Square Stations.
LOCATION on main street; car parking
FOOD breakfast
PRICE rooms $$ with breakfast
ROOMS 15; all have bath or shower, air-conditioning, phone, TV
FACILITIES dining room, 2 sitting rooms
SMOKING no
CREDIT CARDS AE, MC, V
CHILDREN not suitable
DISABLED not suitable
CLOSED never
PROPRIETOR Ellen Riley

MASSACHUSETTS

CHATHAM

CAPTAIN'S HOUSE INN
~ SEA-CAPTAIN'S HOME ~

369-377 Old Harbor Road, Chatham, Cape Cod, MA 02633
TEL (508) 9450127; (800) 3150728 FAX (508) 9450866
E-MAIL info@captainshouseinn.com WEBSITE www.captainshouse.com

CHATHAM IS LOCATED right on the 'elbow' of Cape Cod and has a year-round community made up of fishermen, artists and retired folk from all over the United States. It is named for the town in Britain, and has a feel reminiscent of an English village. That is what attracted Anglo-American couple Jan and Dave McMaster when they were looking for an inn to buy, having worked together already, running a country pub in England.

British pubs, however, do not have plush furnishings and a sophisticated, rather formal atmosphere. Except for afternoon tea with scones, everything here is traditionally American. Beds are either brass or four-poster, floors are thickly-carpeted or of 'pumpkin pine' and wallpapers are Colonial patterns. The house was built in 1839 by sea-captain Hiram Harding and the room named for him is particularly large, with wood panels, ceiling beams and a working fireplace. The McMasters are always innovating. The Hannah Rebekah Room now has a European-style double shower, while the Cambridge and Clarissa Rooms have been reconformed to create the spectacular Clarissa Suite, just as the Challenger and Dauntless Rooms have been combined to make the glamorous Eliza Jane Suite.

~

NEARBY National Wildlife Refuge, beaches.
LOCATION edge of Chatham; car parking
FOOD breakfast
PRICE rooms $$$-$$$$ with breakfast
ROOMS 16; all have bath or shower, air-conditioning, phone, radio, hairdrier
FACILITIES dining room, sitting room; garden
SMOKING no
CREDIT CARDS AE, MC, V
CHILDREN over 12
DISABLED 1 room
CLOSED never
PROPRIETORS Jan and Dave McMaster

MASSACHUSETTS

EAST ORLEANS

NAUSET HOUSE

~ COUNTRY BED-AND-BREAKFAST ~

143 Beach Road, East Orleans, MA 02643
TEL (508) 2552195 FAX (508) 2406276
E-MAIL info@nausethouseinn.com WEBSITE www.nausethouseinn.com

AL AND DIANE JOHNSON, with their daughter Cindy and son-in-law, John Vesella, bought this 1810 farmhouse in 1982. Even now, this is still a relaxed, homey place ... not for those expecting designer decoration or whirlpool tubs. The sitting-room has a lived-in look with sofas and chairs much-used for reading, chatting and even napping. Of the nine bedrooms in the main house, only three have private bathrooms. Rosebud is one, with a white iron bed, a private deck and views into the 100-year-old apple trees below. There is also a carriage house with four bigger bedrooms, which do have en suite facilities, as does the recently renovated Outermost House. This cottage, out in the orchard, is much in demand for honeymoons.

Mother and daughter, both artists, have decorated and stencilled rooms, painting Canada Geese here, a tiny mouse there. Ginger pancakes are a favourite on the cooked breakfast menu, served at the communal table. Guests have the run of the large garden, as well as the century-old conservatory with its weeping cherry and white wicker chairs. Nauset Beach, one of the best on Cape Cod, is just down the road.

~

NEARBY beach, wildlife refuge, cycling; antique shops.
LOCATION east of town; car parking
FOOD breakfast
PRICE rooms $-$$ with breakfast
ROOMS 15; 7 have bath or shower
FACILITIES dining room, sitting room, conservatory; garden
SMOKING no
CREDIT CARDS MC, V
CHILDREN over 12
DISABLED not suitable
CLOSED Nov to March
PROPRIETORS Al and Diane Johnson, Cindy and John Vessella

MASSACHUSETTS

EASTHAM

WHALEWALK

~ WHALING CAPTAIN'S HOUSE ~

220 Bridge Road, Eastham, MA 02642
TEL (508) 2550617; (800) 4401281 FAX (508) 2400017
E-MAIL information@whalewalkinn.com WEBSITE www.whalewalkinn.com

AFTER TEN OUTSTANDING YEARS, the Smiths have moved on. In 2001, the Conlins took over what has long been regarded as one of the best inns on Cape Cod. Carolyn Smith's natural design flair shows in the rooms, which remain light and airy, with wide pine floors and soft, floral colours. Prints are used with restraint, perhaps a stencilled border or a pretty quilt to accentuate the overall colour scheme, which is different in every room. The artwork is of Cape Cod scenes, mainly by local artists.

With a large garden, guests do not feel confined to their rooms. They can help themselves to ice and glasses and use the refrigerator in the pantry. As well as the main house, there are four more buildings: the Barn, the luxurious Carriage House, the Guest House and the Salt Box Cottage, perfect for honeymoon solitude. Some bedrooms have connecting doors, making them useful for family groups. The suites have kitchens and there are some fireplaces and private patios. Breakfasts are imaginative, with pancakes a speciality. Located near the Orleans town line, the Cape Cod Rail Trail cycle path and First Encounter Beach are close by. We welcome reports on the new ownership.

~

NEARBY water sports, cycling; bird sanctuary; antique shops.
LOCATION in residential area; car parking
FOOD breakfast
PRICE rooms $$-$$$ with breakfast
ROOMS 16; all have bath or shower, radio
FACILITIES 2 sitting rooms; terrace, garden
SMOKING no
CREDIT CARDS MC, V
CHILDREN over 12
DISABLED not suitable
CLOSED mid-Dec to mid-Feb
INNKEEPERS Elaine and Kevin Conlin

MASSACHUSETTS

IPSWICH

INN AT CASTLE HILL

~ LUXURY SEASIDE INN ~

280 Argilla Rd, Ipswich, MA 01938
TEL (978) 4122555 FAX (978) 4122556
E-MAIL theinn@castlehill.com WEBSITE www.theinnatcastlehill.com

THIS INN IS AN EXCITING addition to this guide. Start with the location: on a hillside, with stunning views over marshlands to the Atlantic Ocean and surrounded by the 2,100-acre Crane Estate. Guests can play lord and lady of the manor, enjoying the wildlife refuge, 4-mile long beach, gardens and woods before and after the paying public have gone home. (The focal point of the estate is the Great House, a stately home dating from 1928, but it has limited opening hours.)

Staying here is like staying with wealthy friends who have immaculate taste. The decoration follows the 'less is more' philosophy, with contemporary prints, restful colours, and none of the clutter seen in many inns. Cornelius, the master bedroom, has the most spectacular views, but we would happily stay in a smaller room. Breakfasts are delicious (hot dishes a la carte) and served in a sunny corner room. Afternoon tea is taken in the sitting-room, by the fireplace, or out on the large veranda. There are newspapers but no televisions. Unusually, profits from the inn go to a Massachusetts land conservation organisation, so staying here benefits a good cause.

~

NEARBY Newburyport, Gloucester, Rockport, Salem.
LOCATION on estate; car parking
FOOD breakfast, tea
PRICE rooms $$$-$$$$ with breakfast, afternoon tea
ROOMS 10 double; all have bath or shower, air-conditioning, phone, hairdrier
FACILITIES dining room, sitting room; porch, garden, beach
SMOKING no
CREDIT CARDS AE, MC, V
CHILDREN over 12
DISABLED 1 room
CLOSED Jan
MANAGER George Shattuck III

MASSACHUSETTS

LENOX

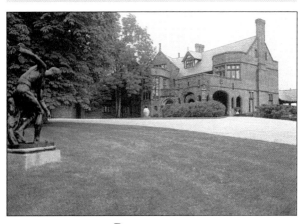

BLANTYRE

~ LUXURY COUNTRY HOUSE ~

Blantyre Road, Lenox, MA 01240
TEL (413) 6373556 FAX (413) 6374282
E-MAIL hide@blantyre.com WEBSITE www.blantyre.com

THIS IS ONE OF THE 'COTTAGES', or summer homes, built by millionaires at the turn-of-the 20th century. It was restored in the early 1980s by Jack and Jane Fitzpatrick, the owners of the Red Lion at Stockbridge. If you have ever wondered how the Carnegies, Astors and Vanderbilts lived, all you need is a large bank balance and you can find out. An 18-page 'house history' tells the tales of this imposing imitation of a Scottish castle. Ground-floor rooms are of heroic, Gothic proportions and furnishings are suitably grand: a tapestry hangs in the panelled dining room; a Steinway grand piano stands in the music room.

The atmosphere is formal, "your suitcase should contain tennis whites, jackets and ties for gentlemen, smart outfits for ladies," advises our inspector. The dining room, with fine linen and crystal, bone china and cutlery, is open to the public. Chef Christopher Brooks prepares sophisticated modern dishes: seared *foie gras* with pear pureé and *ahi* tuna with *tabbouleh*. The bedrooms are less sombre than the reception rooms, with 'four-poster beds that would defy the princess to notice the pea'. Three cottages are hidden in the grounds.

~

NEARBY Tanglewood, Hancock Shaker Village; golf.
LOCATION large estate; car parking
FOOD breakfast, lunch in summer, dinner
PRICE rooms $$$$ with breakfast
ROOMS 23; all have bath or shower
FACILITIES 2 dining rooms; terrace, garden, swimming pool, tennis
SMOKING restricted
CREDIT CARDS AE, DC, MC, V
CHILDREN over 12
DISABLED not suitable
CLOSED Nov to mid-May
MANAGER Katja Henke

MASSACHUSETTS

LENOX

THE GABLES INN

~ HISTORIC HOME ~

81 Walker Street, Lenox, MA 01240
TEL (413) 6373416; (800) 3829401 FAX (413) 6373416
WEBSITE www.gableslenox.com

WRITER EDITH WHARTON (*The Age of Innocence*) is part of the romance that is Lenox. Bored by Newport society, she decided to summer here in the Berkshires, spending time at Pine Acre, her mother-in-law's house, before moving to The Mount nearby. Today that Queen Anne-style 'cottage' is the white Gables Inn, with striped awnings and red shutters. The Edith Wharton connection is heavily promoted by the owners Frank and Mary Newton who have a show business background.

Guests can sit in the author's (recreated) octagonal library or sleep in the four-poster bed in her flowery room. Other bedrooms are just as carefully decorated: the President's room, with its photographs, autographs and ephemera devoted to America's leaders; the Teddy Wharton suite, with dark green striped wallpaper and a leather sofa, vry much a man's room.

The day begins in the rather boardroom-like breakfast room. After that, guests can look through the Newton's collection of Broadway memorabilia or request a record from a show. There are also the tennis court, glassed-in swimming pool, terrace and garden for relaxing.

~

NEARBY Tanglewood, theatre, dance; golf, winter sports.
LOCATION in town; car parking
FOOD breakfast
PRICE rooms $$-$$$ with breakfast
ROOMS 19; all have bath or shower, air-conditioning
FACILITIES dining room, sitting room; terrace, indoor swimming pool
SMOKING restricted
CREDIT CARDS MC, V
CHILDREN over 12
DISABLED not suitable
CLOSED never
PROPRIETORS Frank and Mary Newton

MASSACHUSETTS

LENOX

GARDEN GABLES INN

~ BED-AND BREAKFAST ~

PO Box 52, 135 Main Street, Lenox, MA 01240
TEL (413) 6370193 FAX (413) 6374554
E-MAIL gardeninn@aol.com WEBSITE www.lenoxinn.com

N OT TO BE CONFUSED with The Gables, also in Lenox. This is near the middle of town, but secluded in its own grounds. An intriguing puzzle of architectural geometry, it has gambrel roof lines mixed with steep gables and shuttered dormer windows, all in white with green trim. Flowers along the paths provide accents of colour. Although the estate dates from 1780, this has only been an inn for 50 years. When Canadians Mario and Lynn Mekinda took over in 1988 they upgraded the rambling building, doing much of the carpentry and wallpapering themselves. Their style is informal; they want guests to feel at home, using the kitchen and refrigerator and helping themselves to tea and coffee all day.

Some stays are for four or five weeks in summer, thanks, no doubt, to the 25 m pool. There are two sitting rooms: one for peace and quiet, the other with television and piano. The main house has many twists, turns and low ceilings. Bedrooms of all shapes and sizes are simply furnished. The cottage rooms are appealing: number 19, with a cathedral ceiling, has a contemporary feel with Shaker-style furnishings and woodwork. Breakfast is a communal affair, served buffet-style.

~

NEARBY Tanglewood, theatre festivals; golf, winter sports.
LOCATION in Lenox; car parking
FOOD breakfast
PRICE rooms $$-$$$ with breakfast
ROOMS 18 double; all have bath or shower; air-conditioning, phone, TV
FACILITIES dining room, 2 sitting rooms; terrace, garden, swimming pool
SMOKING restricted
CREDIT CARDS MC, V
CHILDREN over 12
DISABLED not suitable
CLOSED never
PROPRIETORS Lynn and Mario Mekinda

MASSACHUSETTS

LENOX

WALKER HOUSE

~ TOWN HOUSE ~

74 Walker Street, Lenox, MA 01240
TEL (413) 6371271; (800) 2353098 FAX (413) 6372387
E-MAIL phoudek@vgernet.net WEBSITE www.walkerhouse.com

LENOX IS FAMOUS FOR attracting music lovers throughout the summer months, but the Houdeks decided to live here all year. Richard (music critic) and Peggy (opera singer) left their native California, bought the elegant Federal-style house and turned it into an inn only minutes from Tanglewood. Appropriately, bedrooms are named after composers such as Chopin, Beethoven and Mozart. Handel, at the front of the house, has a fine brass bed that could almost double as a baroque musical instrument.

When our inspector arrived, guests were lingering over breakfast on the long, wide veranda, with its wicker rocker and jungle of plants. Inside, more plants as well as cats battle for attention among the antiques. Some inns have rather serious atmospheres. The Houdeks have flair as well as a sense of humour: along the stairs are whimsical paintings of cats in circus costumes. In the evening, operas and movies are shown on a giant television screen and this enthusiastic couple also encourages young talent by hosting the occasional recital.

There are peaceful woods behind, several restaurants within walking distance, and free bicycles.

~

NEARBY Tanglewood, theatre, dance; golf, winter sports.
LOCATION in town; car parking
FOOD breakfast, snacks
PRICE rooms $-$$$
ROOMS 8 double; all have bath or shower
FACILITIES dining room, sitting room; garden
SMOKING no
CREDIT CARDS not accepted
CHILDREN over 12
DISABLED not suitable
CLOSED never
PROPRIETORS Richard and Peggy Houdek

MASSACHUSETTS

LENOX

WHEATLEIGH

~ LUXURY MANSION ~

Hawthorne Road, Lenox MA 01240
TEL (413) 6370610 FAX (413) 6374507
E-MAIL info@wheatleigh.com WEBSITE www.wheatleigh.com

"TRADE THE MAPLES AND PINES for cypress and cedar and this could be a hillside palace in Tuscany," was one European guest's reaction. Located next door to Tanglewood, Wheatleigh was inspired by Italian *palazzos* and built by Italian craftsmen. The entrance hall has the look, ambience and hush of an art museum. An impeccably-tailored waiter glides upstairs with a silver ice bucket and bottle of Veuve Clicquot. Contemporary sculptures blend with museum-quality 17thC and 18thC antiques and details such as bas relief carving and stained-glass windows.

Surprisingly, the bedrooms are restrained with muted colours, few patterns and a total lack of clutter. Views stretch across the sculpture garden to the Berkshire hills. There is a range of prices but the 'standard' rooms are surprisingly good value for money. The restaurant is grand and formal, but Chef Peter Platt's cooking is modern: grilled swordfish with a hot and sour sauce and tropical fruit compote; crab flan with asparagus, *morels* and white truffle vinaigrette. Prices are New York City, but so is the service. There is a swimming pool and a tennis court and, most telling of all, owners Mr and Mrs Simon appear daily.

~

NEARBY Tanglewood, theatres, museums, antique shops.
LOCATION in Lenox; car parking
FOOD breakfast, dinner
PRICE rooms $$-$$$$; charge for breakfast
ROOMS 19; all have bath or shower, air-conditioning, phone; some fireplaces
FACILITIES dining room, sitting room; terrace, garden, swimming pool
SMOKING restricted
CREDIT CARDS AE, DC, MC, V
CHILDREN not suitable
DISABLED not suitable
CLOSED never
GENERAL MANAGER François Thomas

MASSACHUSETTS

MARTHA'S VINEYARD

CHARLOTTE INN
~ LUXURY INN ~

South Summer Street, Edgartown, MA 02539
TEL (508) 6274751 FAX (508) 6274652
E-MAIL charlotte@relaischateaux.com WEBSITE www.relaischateaux.fr

A MEMBER OF the Relais & Châteaux group, this is one of the best-known inns in New England. Set in the heart of Edgartown, whose historic houses could be a film set for a costume drama, the hotel spreads over five buildings. The oldest dates from 1705; the largest is a 19thC merchant's house. Some say it looks like a museum; we liken it to an English country house hotel. Gary Conover is passionate about collecting antiques and not just furniture and prints. There are old umbrellas, hats, suitcases, even fishing creels, all placed as if ready for use in a private home. Bedrooms vary in size but have every comfort: number 17 in the Summer House has a high brass bed, a television hidden in a cupboard, a 1930s telephone and a big bathroom with plenty of thick towels and a bathtub large enough to soak in.

L'Etoile, the restaurant, has a high reputation for sophisticated dishes using foie-gras, venison, lobster and pheasant, 'jackets for gentlemen' is the request. After three decades of innkeeping, Gary has more firm opinions; there are no weddings, reunions or conferences, "because they would disturb our other guests". Rating: expensive but worth it for an extra-special occasion.

~

NEARBY restaurants, shops; bicycle rental; harbour.
LOCATION in historic district; public car parking
FOOD breakfast, lunch, dinner
PRICE rooms $$-$$$$ with breakfast
ROOMS 23; all have bath or shower, radio; air-conditioning, phone, TV
FACILITIES 2 dining rooms, 3 sitting rooms; terrace, garden
SMOKING restricted
CREDIT CARDS AE, MC, V
CHILDREN over 14
DISABLED not suitable
CLOSED never
PROPRIETORS Gary and Paula Conover

MASSACHUSETTS

MARTHA'S VINEYARD

MARTHA'S PLACE

~ BED-AND-BREAKFAST INN ~

Address of hotel
TEL (508) 6930253
E-MAIL marthas@vineyard.net WEBSITE www.marthasplace.com

VINEYARD HAVEN is the year-round ferry port for the island and, although it now has upmarket clothing and gift shops, the village atmosphere remains. The theatre and old-fashioned movie house thrive and locals still meet up to chat over coffee and the morning paper. A five-minute walk away from the shops and restaurants is Martha's Place, a handsome 1840 Greek Revival house with a fine garden and views of the harbour and boats. The inn has the antiques, polished floors and carefully chosen fabrics that we expect of one of the best romantic getaways on the Vineyard. But hosts Richard Alcott and Martin Hicks provide even more. Included in the price are: tennis racquets and balls to use on the nearby clay courts, mountain bicycles for exploring the island, beach chairs, towels and coolers for picnics. Bedrooms even have stamped postcards and an 'overnight kit' with toothbrush and paste, shaving cream and razor. Owen Park, a public beach, is a short walk away. Breakfast is communal and served at a long table set with china and silver; or, you can have a tray brought up to your room. Remember, however, the checkout time is early: 10am.

~

NEARBY beaches, fishing, water-sports, harbour, lighthouse.
LOCATION in residential area; car parking
FOOD breakfast
PRICE rooms $$-$$$$ with breakfast
ROOMS 6 double; family; all have bath or shower, air-conditioning, phone, radio, TV, CD player, data ports; some Jacuzzi, working fireplaces, hairdrier
FACILITIES dining room, sitting room; porch, garden
SMOKING no
CREDIT CARDS AE, MC, V
CHILDREN not suitable
DISABLED not suitable
CLOSED never
PROPRIETORS Martin Hicks and Richard Alcott

MASSACHUSETTS

MARTHA'S VINEYARD

LAMBERT'S COVE COUNTRY INN

∽ RESTAURANT-INN ∽

Lambert's Cove Road, West Tisbury; write to: RR1, Box 442, Vineyard Haven MA 02568
TEL (508) 6932298 FAX (508) 6937890
E-MAIL lambinn@gis.net WEBSITE www.lambertscoveinn.com

IN THIS PART OF THE ISLAND, the low stone walls, gentle hills and woods look like the countryside west of Boston; then, suddenly there are views over the water. This 18thC farmhouse stands in a secluded setting inland, though, with a popular restaurant open to the public, it is not exactly a hideaway. Small business meetings are hosted, as are weddings, particularly in the spring, when the apple orchard, huge wisteria and lilac are in bloom. There is an all-weather tennis court and access to nearby Lambert's Cove Beach, usually open only to town residents.

Comfortable sofas, wing chairs, and fireplaces create a comfortable 'country' ambience. The spacious library has shelves of books, plus games, puzzles and a writing desk; doors open into the garden. The carriage house and barn are across the lawn, so rooms here have more privacy. Open to the public, the restaurant is a long-time island favourite, serving straightforward dishes, such as rack of lamb, duck breast and veal piccata, as well as more imaginative ones, such as lobster bolognese. In 2001, Liz Macfarlane returned to manage her mother's inn, and she promises no major changes.

∽

NEARBY beaches, nature reserve, water sports.
LOCATION off country road; car parking
FOOD breakfast, dinner
PRICE rooms $$-$$$ with breakfast
ROOMS 15 double; all have bath or shower, radio
FACILITIES dining room, 2 sitting rooms; deck, garden, tennis court
SMOKING restricted
CREDIT CARDS AE, MC, V
CHILDREN over 8
DISABLED not suitable
CLOSED never
MANAGER Liz Macfarlane

MASSACHUSETTS

MARTHA'S VINEYARD

THE OUTERMOST INN

~ COASTAL INN ~

RR1, Box 171, Lighthouse Road, Gay Head, MA 02535
TEL (508) 6453511 FAX (508) 6453514
E-MAIL inquiries@outermostinn.com WEBSITE www.outermostinn.com

HUGH AND JEANNE TAYLOR are independent types, so it is no surprise that their inn is at the western tip of the island, away from the summer crowds. They designed and built this house themselves thirty years ago, then added on to it and opened to guests in 1989. Views are over water, across dunes and to the Gay Head light house.

Where most inns in New England have antiques and walls painted in Colonial colours or papered with Victorian-style prints, this is unfussy, stylish and modern. Bedrooms are named for the woods used: Ash, Beech and B-Ash, a mixture of the two. Instead of curtains, windows have white venetian blinds "for better ventilation". Walls are plain, artwork is contemporary and bathrooms are streamlined, with first-class lighting. The bar on the long porch is half of a tree-trunk.

Hugh, the brother of singer-songwriter James Taylor, sometimes plays the piano or guitar. Jeanne serves the full breakfast; non-residents may book in for dinner. Surrounded by a nature reserve, there is plenty of wildlife, from osprey and falcons to deer and skunk. Beaches are minutes away. Hugh also offers trips on his catamaran.

~

NEARBY beaches, cycling, sailing.
LOCATION on country road; car parking
FOOD breakfast, dinner
PRICE rooms $$$-$$$$
ROOMS 7; all have bath or shower; TV by request
FACILITIES dining room, sitting room, bar; porch, garden
SMOKING no
CREDIT CARDS AE, MC, V
CHILDREN not suitable
DISABLED not suitable
CLOSED Nov to April; restaurant only, Wed
PROPRIETORS Jeanne and Hugh Taylor

MASSACHUSETTS

MARTHA'S VINEYARD

SHIVERICK INN

~ VICTORIAN BED-AND-BREAKFAST ~

PO Box 640, Edgartown, MA 02539
TEL (508) 6273797; (800) 7234292 FAX (508) 6278441
E-MAIL shiverickinn@vineyard.net WEBSITE www.shiverickinn.com

IN 2000, Paul Weiss purchased this 150-year-old mansion. He added a baby grand piano and his own selection of antiques to those left by the previous owners, the Turmelles. So, regulars can request number 6, knowing that the king-size, carved bed with lace drapery remains. Number 10 still has its balcony with views of the garden and the steeple of the Old Whaling Church. Despite the maritime history of the island, this was not the home of a sea-captain or a merchant; it was built for a Dr Shiverick.

Downstairs, there is a real feeling of space, from the large entrance hall to the sitting-room, with its squashy sofa in front of the fireplace and handsome mahogany sideboard. A full breakfast is now served, with three or four sorts of freshly baked breads and coffee cakes, as well as a hot entrée. Afternoon tea is another highlight, served out on the patio in summer. Colours in the bedrooms are generally deep, such as mulberry, pine green or dark blue; the random-width, original floorboards remain. Although some rooms are quite small, all have bathrobes. We liked the relaxed atmosphere. Located in the historic district, this is just a short walk from the harbour.

~

NEARBY restaurants, shops; bicycle rental.
LOCATION in town; car parking
FOOD breakfast
PRICE rooms $$-$$$ with breakfast
ROOMS 9 double; 1 suite; all have bath or shower, air-conditioning
FACILITIES dining room, sitting room; terrace, garden
SMOKING no
CREDIT CARDS AE, MC, V
CHILDREN over 12
DISABLED not suitable
CLOSED never
MANAGER Kristin Allen

MASSACHUSETTS

MARTHA'S VINEYARD

THORNCROFT INN

〜 BED-AND-BREAKFAST INN 〜

Main Street, Vineyard Haven, MA 02568
TEL (508) 6933333; (800) 3321236 FAX (508) 6935419
E-MAIL innkeeper@thorncroft.com WEBSITE www.thorncroft.com

EVERYTHING HERE is designed to provide a romantic getaway for couples. There are no spare beds to put in rooms, televisions have wireless headphones to eliminate 'noise pollution' and you can have a continental breakfast brought to your room. If you want a full meal, that is served in the dining room in two sittings: 8.15 or 9.30 am, with a hot dish such as eggs or pancakes.

From the street, this could be just another pleasant suburban house and it still feels like a private home, with no reception desk and a rather small sitting room and sunroom. Lynn and Karl Buder have been innkeepers since 1980. Their style is friendly but low-key, like their choice of decoration: traditional patterns and antique or reproduction furniture. Four-poster, canopy beds, fireplaces and private hot tubs or Jacuzzis are available but not in every room. All, however, have fresh towels each evening, an iron and ironing board, and an ice bucket with bottle opener and wine glasses. There is a refrigerator for guests' use; bicycles may be stored in the garage. Those wanting more seclusion should opt for the rooms in the converted carriage house in the large garden. The non-smoking rule is a strict one.

〜

NEARBY West Chop lighthouse; beaches; ferry; bicycle rental.
LOCATION in residential area; car parking
FOOD breakfast
PRICE rooms $$$-$$$$ with breakfast
ROOMS 14; all have bath or shower, air-conditioning, phone, TV, radio, hairdrier
FACILITIES dining room, 2 sitting rooms; garden
SMOKING no
CREDIT CARDS AE, DC, MC, V
CHILDREN not suitable
DISABLED 1 room
CLOSED never
PROPRIETORS Lynn and Karl Buder

MASSACHUSETTS

NANTUCKET

SHERBURNE INN
~ ISLAND BED-AND-BREAKFAST ~

10 Gay Street, Nantucket, MA 02554
TEL (508) 2284425; (888) 5774425 FAX (508) 2288114
E-MAIL sherinn@nantucket.net WEBSITE www.sherburneinn.com

NANTUCKET IS FURTHER out in the Atlantic Ocean than Martha's
Vineyard and has only one small town. There is no need to take a
car; visitors walk or rent bicycles. Taxis provide transport to outer points
of the island. Settled by Quakers in 1659, Nantucket's fame came from
whaling. Nowadays, it is known for its 'quaint' old cobbled streets, grey-
shingle buildings and boat-filled harbour. Neon signs and fast food
restaurants are banned.

On their first visit to Nantucket, Dale Hamilton and Susan Gasparich
decided to buy this inn. They upgraded the furnishings, putting in pretty
wallpapers that look more 'private home' than 'interior decorator'. Rooms
here come in different sizes and there is no dining-room. "That's because
it was built as a silk factory, not a sea captain's or merchant's home,"
according to Susan. So, the continental breakfast is served in the sitting-
room; some guests stay to chat, others eat on the deck or in the privacy of
their rooms. That 'make yourself at home' feeling is part of the appeal here
and it reflects the relaxed yet professional attitude of the innkeepers.

~

NEARBY beaches, fishing, water-sports; bicycle rental.
LOCATION in town; car parking on street
FOOD breakfast
PRICE rooms $-$$$$ with breakfaster
ROOMS 8 double; all have bath or shower, air-conditioning, phone, TV, hairdrier
FACILITIES 2 sitting rooms; deck, garden
SMOKING no
CREDIT CARDS AE, MC, V
CHILDREN over 6
DISABLED not suitable
CLOSED never
PROPRIETORS Susan Gasparich and Dale Hamilton

MASSACHUSETTS

THE WAUWINET

~ LUXURY SEASIDE INN ~

Wauwinet Road, Nantucket MA 02584
TEL (508) 2280145; (800) 4268718 FAX (508) 2286712
E-MAIL email@wauwinet.com WEBSITE www.wauwinet.com

THE SUMMER CROWDS of the town of Nantucket are twenty minutes away by car from this spit of land between the bay and the Atlantic Ocean. A century ago, fishermen would stop here for hot meals. Then it was just a shack; now this is one of the most expensive hotels in this guide. You might, therefore, expect a formal atmosphere, ostentatious decoration and flunkies waiting to be ordered about. You'd be wrong. This is a 'get away from it all' place where the overall simplicity belies a deep comfort. Bedrooms are full of delicate colours; the look throughout is spacious, light and airy.

Toppers, the restaurant, has a high reputation and is open to the public. Chef Chais Freeman is a superstar in New England. Dishes range from roast muscovy duck to lobster, sautéed, and served with a champagne beurre blanc, followed by poached pears and caramel sauce. Manager Russ Cleveland lectures on the whaling era and leads nature walks.

There are tennis courts, a croquet lawn, kayaks, sailing and row boats. These, plus mountain bikes and boat or bus transport into town, are included in the price. Is it worth it? Regulars come year after year, even several times a summer.

~

NEARBY water-sports, cycle paths, nature reserve; beaches.
LOCATION out of town; car parking
FOOD breakfast, lunch, dinner
PRICE rooms $$$$ with breakfast
ROOMS 26; all have bath or shower, air-conditioning, phone, TV
FACILITIES dining room, sitting room, bar; garden
SMOKING no
CREDIT CARDS AE, DC, MC, V
CHILDREN over 12
DISABLED 2 rooms
CLOSED Nov to Aril
MANAGERS Bettinn and Eric Landt

MASSACHUSETTS

PROVINCETOWN

THE COPPER FOX

~ 19THC BED-AND-BREAKFAST ~

448 Commercial Street, Provincetown, MA 02657
TEL (508) 4878583 FAX (508) 4873238
E-MAIL copperfox@provincetown.com WEBSITE www.provincetown.com/copperfox

PROVINCETOWN, at the tip of Cape Cod, boasts that the Pilgrim Fathers landed here in 1620. Later, whaling was a major industry; now visitors go whale watching. It was a 19thC artists' colony, and the bohemian atmosphere persists, with a relaxed gay community. But Provincetown caters for all, year-round. Some head for the shops and art galleries; others climb the Pilgrim Monument for the view, then make for the unspoiled beaches, part of the Cape Cod National Seashore. Thankfully this is a quiet, well-run bed-and-breakfast in what can be a busy town. The house belonged to a sea captain, respected enough to have the street outside named after him. The 1856 building has been upgraded by the addition of a wraparound porch, a conservatory and a sunroom. The surrounding lawns are ideal for lazing about.

All the rooms are different. Some guests favour the Bay suites, with views over Provincetown Bay. Others insist on the Garden Suite, with its own tiny garden, or the Studio Apartment that sleeps six. Both have their own entrances and kitchenettes for longer stays. Furnishing is pretty without being fussy. Breakfast, with muffins and breads, is a delight out on the porch in summer.

~

NEARBY shops, art galleries, beach, harbour; bicycle rental.
LOCATION in town; car parking
FOOD breakfast
PRICE rooms $-$$$ with breakfast
ROOMS 7; all have bath or shower, air-conditioning
FACILITIES dining room; garden
SMOKING no
CREDIT CARDS AE, MC, V
CHILDREN over 12
DISABLED not suitable CLOSED never
PROPRIETOR John Gagliardi

MASSACHUSETTS

PROVINCETOWN

SNUG COTTAGE

~ HILLTOP BED-AND-BREAKFAST ~

178 Bradford Street, Provincetown, MA 02657
TEL (508) 4871616; (800) 4322334 FAX (508) 4875596
E-MAIL snugcottage@usa.net WEBSITE www.snugcottage.com

LET'S ELIMINATE some confusion. This used to be called the Bradford Gardens before James Mack and Paul Gizara took over in 2000. Previously, they ran a smaller inn in town, also called Snug Cottage, and they brought the name with them. This 1825 clapboard house sits on a hilltop, looking across a street to the Atlantic Ocean. All round is a large garden with a huge Japanese cherry tree plus roses and oriental lilies.

Inside, the revamped bedrooms are named for great Brits, such as Churchill and Victoria, "because Paul is a hopeless Anglophile." The bathrooms are much improved, spare beds have been removed to create more sitting space, but air-conditioning, telephones and data ports have been added. Thankfully, rooms remain well priced. The dining room has also been restored, so that guests have plenty of space at breakfast time. Paul is a Culinary Institute of American-trained chef who rustles up New England dishes that great grandmas would be proud of: peach spoon bread and blueberry buckle. We like the early morning coffee, the library of books, and drinks before going to dinner.

~

NEARBY shopping; beaches, cycling, whale watching.
LOCATION in residential area; car parking
FOOD breakfast
PRICE rooms $$-$$$ with breakfast
ROOMS 8 double; all have bath or shower, TV, radio
FACILITIES sitting room; garden
SMOKING no
CREDIT CARDS AE, MC, V
CHILDREN over 10
DISABLED not suitable
CLOSED never
INNKEEPERS James Mack, Paul Gizara

MASSACHUSETTS

ROCKPORT

YANKEE CLIPPER

~ SEASIDE INN ~

127 Granite Street, Rockport, MA 01966
TEL (978) 5463407; (800) 5453699 FAX (978) 5469730
E-MAIL info@yankeeclipperinn.com WEBSITE www.yankeeclipperinn.com

CAPE ANN PROJECTS from Boston's North Shore into the Atlantic Ocean and Rockport, long known as a 'picturesque' fishing village and artists' colony, is busy all summer long. In 2000, Cathy and Randy Marks took over from the Ellis family, who had run this inn for two generations. Although they have made some changes, they plan to keep the relaxing atmosphere.

The most obvious draw here is the setting: on a rocky bluff with wide views east across the Atlantic Ocean or south to the boat-filled harbour. There are chairs on the broad, sloping lawns and a heated swimming-pool. The original mansion dates from 1929, though the dark wood has a Victorian look. Some of the bedrooms have private balconies, four share the rooftop deck. The size varies but all are comfortable and pleasant, with antiques or wicker furniture and pretty patterns. Bedrooms in the Quarterdeck, in the garden, have a contemporary look. Unlike many bed-and-breakfast inns, the Marks welcome children; "after all, we have three of our own". They no longer offer dinner, but restaurants are nearby. Remember that Rockport is a 'dry' town, so you must take your own wine.

~

NEARBY whale watching, sailing, fishing.
LOCATION on the ocean; car parking
FOOD breakfast
PRICE rooms $$-$$$$ with breakfast
ROOMS 16; all have bath or shower, air-conditioning, phone, radio, hairdrier
FACILITIES dining room, 2 sitting rooms; garden, swimming-pool
SMOKING no
CREDIT CARDS AE, MC, V
CHILDREN very welcome
DISABLED not suitable
CLOSED Jan, Feb
PROPRIETORS Randy and Cathy Marks

MASSACHUSETTS

SOUTH YARMOUTH

CAPTAIN FARRIS HOUSE

~ SEA-CAPTAIN'S HOME ~

308 Old Main Street, South Yarmouth, MA 02664
TEL (508) 7602818; (800) 3509477 FAX (508) 3981262
E-MAIL thecaptain@captainfarris.com WEBSITE www.captainfarris.com

THIS PART OF CAPE COD is not 'quaint'. It is, however, near the ferries to Nantucket and Martha's Vineyard, to beaches and to summer theatres. Moreover, the town is upgrading the area by buying private property to turn into public parks.

This splendid old house is owned and run by Stephen and Patricia Bronstein. Native New Englanders, originally from New Hampshire, they pride themselves on their professional approach: "We are not doing this as a hobby." Detail is everything, from the three-course, home-cooked breakfasts to the laundry that they do in-house to ensure that the linens are fresher than fresh. Patricia bakes cinnamon apple sour cream muffins, then conjures up ham and cheese herbed frittatas. The four suites and six double rooms have been upgraded and redecorated in the past five years, in what is an on-going process. All but one have two-person Jacuzzis. The favourite room with readers is the Phoebe White suite on the top floor of the separate 1825 Elisha Jenkins House. Not surprisingly, the inn is busy year-round: "The only thing you can't do in the fall and winter on the Cape is swim."

~

NEARBY golf, fishing, beaches; ferries; shopping; theatres.
LOCATION on quiet street; car parking
FOOD breakfast
PRICE rooms $$-$$$ with breakfast
ROOMS 10; all have bath or shower, phone, TV, radio, hairdrier
FACILITIES dining room, sitting room; porch, garden
SMOKING no
CREDIT CARDS AE, MC, V
CHILDREN over 12
DISABLED not suitable
CLOSED never
PROPRIETORS Stephen and Patricia Bronstein

MASSACHUSETTS

STOCKBRIDGE

THE INN AT STOCKBRIDGE

~ LUXURY INN ~

Route 7, Box 618, Stockbridge, MA 01262
TEL (413) 2983337: (888) 4667865 FAX (413) 2983406
E-MAIL innkeeper@stockbridgeinn.com WEBSITE www.stockbridgeinn.com

THIS SHOULD BE the Inn near Stockbridge, since the turn-of-the-century, mock-Georgina house is separated from the attractive town by the Massachusetts Turnpike. Dating from 1906, this is one of the original 200 'Berkshire cottages' built as summer homes by millionaires.

The Schillers have introduced big changes in recent years, opening the Cottage House in 1997 and the Barn in 1999. Some guests insist on the same room each visit; others want to experience somewhere different. The rooms in the main building are a delight, pretty and traditional, with antiques. The Blagden Suite and South Corner Room have soothing colour schemes and views over lawn, gardens or distant hills. On the ground floor, the Terrace Room opens onto a private patio.

The Cottage House is more modern with gas fires, VCRs and whirlpools, while the Barn has huge rooms, with individual decks and sliding screens. What brings folks back? "Lenny's cottage cheese pancakes. They're always asking for the recipe." Although the highway is quite close, there is no noise inside the inn or around the swimming-pool.

~

NEARBY Tanglewood, Normal Rockwell Museum; golf.
LOCATION outside town; car parking
FOOD breakfast
PRICE rooms $$-$$$$ with breakfast
ROOMS 16 double; all have bath or shower, phone, TV
FACILITIES dining room, sitting room; garden, swimming-pool
SMOKING no
CREDIT CARDS AE, MC, V
CHILDREN over 12
DISABLED 1 room
CLOSED never
OWNERS Alice and Len Schiller

MASSACHUSETTS

COLONEL EBENEZER CRAFTS INN

~ HILLTOP BED-AND-BREAKFAST ~

On the Common, Sturbridge, MA 01566
TEL (508) 3473313; (800) 7825425 FAX (508) 3471246
E-MAIL info@publickhouse.com WEBSITE www.publickhouse.com/ebenezercraftsinn

OLD STURBRIDGE VILLAGE is a recreation of the 1830s. The blacksmith, shoemaker and farmer, along with other 'villagers' in costume, perform and explain their daily tasks to visitors who flock here throughout the year, particularly on weekends. History is big business in Sturbridge.

For those who prefer to get away from the crowds, this bed-and-breakfast stands high on a ridge above the town. Built as a farmhouse in 1786, it feels more spacious than many homes from that period. Behind a cupboard is the bricked-up entrance to a tunnel, part of the 19thC 'underground railway', that helped slaves from the South escape to freedom in the North. Although comfortable and attractive, this has not been 'designer-decorated'; the furniture is traditional but there are no priceless antiques. The large sitting room extends into the original kitchen and also into a sun room on the side. Bedrooms are pretty, bathrooms have been upgraded. The cottage, with its own entrance, is particularly suitable for families. There is a swimming pool in the garden. Reservations are made through the sister inn, the bigger, always busy Publick House in Sturbridge.

~

NEARBY Old Sturbridge village.
LOCATION above Sturbridge; car parking
FOOD breakfast
PRICE rooms $-$$ with breakfast
ROOMS 6 double; 1 suite; 1 family; all have bath or shower, air-conditioning
FACILITIES dining room, 3 sitting rooms; garden, swimming pool
SMOKING restricted
CREDIT CARDS AE, DC, MC, V
CHILDREN welcome
DISABLED not suitable
CLOSED never
INNKEEPER Albert Cournoyer

MASSACHUSETTS

WEST FALMOUTH

INN AT WEST FALMOUTH
~ LUXURY BED-AND-BREAKFAST ~

PO Box 1208, West Falmouth, MA 02574
TEL (508) 5407696 FAX (508) 5409977

FROM HIGH on Telegraph Hill, this mansion looks down to trees and houses and across to Buzzards Bay. Built in 1898 as a private home, it has the traditional Cape Cod weathered grey shingles trimmed with white. Inside, however, there is none of the Victorian or Colonial 'inn' decoration: this could be a photo-feature in a design magazine. Quality is everywhere from the lemon yellow walls and green printed fabrics in the sitting room to the stained-glass windows in the dining room.

Most of the bedrooms have views of the bay; the others look over the unusually well-landscaped gardens to woods. Most have a working fireplace and a sitting area, but all bathrooms have Italian marble. At the top is the windowed 'widows walk' where guests gather to watch the sun setting into Buzzards Bay. Although there is a swimming pool and a tennis court, this is not the place to bring children. Swathes of expensive fabrics, imported rugs and objets d'art, make this a stylish retreat for adults. The only innovations are hidden: modems for business folk lie behind Waverley curtains. Be careful to get detailed directions and follow them; there are no signs.

~

NEARBY beaches, Cape Cod, ferry to Martha's Vineyard.
LOCATION overlooking bay; car parking
FOOD breakfast
PRICE rooms $$-$$$ with breakfast
ROOMS 8; all have bath or shower, phone, hairdrier, safe
FACILITIES dining room, sitting room; garden, heated swimming pool, tennis court
SMOKING no
CREDIT CARDS AE, MC, V
CHILDREN not suitable
DISABLED not suitable
CLOSED never
INNKEEPER Sue Barry

MASSACHUSETTS

WEST STOCKBRIDGE

WILLIAMSVILLE INN

~ FARMHOUSE INN ~

Route 41, West Stockbridge, MA 01266
TEL (413) 2746118 FAX (413) 2743539
E-MAIL williamsville@taconic.net WEBSITE williamsvilleinn.com

SOMEWHAT OFF THE BEATEN PATH in the Berkshire hills regions of western Massachusetts is this inn, run by a mother-and-daughter team. Standing at the foot of Tom Ball Mountain, it is secluded but not inconvenient for the music, dance and theatrical events. In summer, the meadow becomes an art gallery with a temporary display of sculptures. The extensive grounds also include a swimming pool and a tennis court.

Inside the 1797 house, the wide floorboards and muted colours of sage green and mulberry are typically Colonial. Some houses from this period can feel cramped, but enlargements, such as the greenhouse-style breakfast room, give a feeling of space. A side door leads to the tiny Tavern Room where guests have drinks before dinner. Non-residents may book into the main dining room, with its huge fireplace; menus range from tournedos of beef with wild mushrooms to herb-roasted free range chicken or scallops with vine-ripened tomatoes. Vegetables and herbs, like the flowers on the tables, come from the large gardens. Bedrooms are in the main house, the barn and cottages; some have fireplaces or wood stoves.

~

NEARBY Tanglewood; hiking, cycling; historic houses.
LOCATION on country road; car parking
FOOD breakfast, dinner
PRICE rooms $$-$$$ with breakfast
ROOMS 16 double; all have bath or shower
FACILITIES 4 dining rooms, sitting room, bar; garden, swimming pool, tennis court
SMOKING restricted
CREDIT CARDS AE, MC, V
CHILDREN over 10
DISABLED not suitable
CLOSED never
PROPRIETORS Gail and Kathleen Ryan

MASSACHUSETTS

WEDGEWOOD INN
∽ VILLAGE BED-AND-BREAKFAST ∽

83 Main Street, Yarmouth Port, MA 02675
TEL (508) 3625157
E-MAIL info@wedgewood-inn.com WEBSITE www.wedgewood-inn.com

'THE QUINTESSENTIAL NEW ENGLAND bed-and-breakfast' is how rival innkeepers describe the Wedgewood, run by the Grahams since 1986. Milt is a large man with a gentle manner that belies his past: he played for the Patriots, the professional football team based near Boston, then was an agent with the FBI. Gerrie is more outgoing; a former teacher, she takes pride in her garden, with its gazebo, rhododendrons and flower beds. Guests sit at individual tables for breakfasts, which are straightforward, foregoing the outlandish dishes served in some inns.

This white, clapboard house dates from 1812 and is on the National Register of Historic Places. Rooms have a spacious feel and are full of antiques, like the unusual clock that is built into the wall by the stairs. There are plenty of four-poster beds, fireplaces, patchwork quilts and even some private porches. Wallpapers are traditional and oriental carpets lie on polished floor boards that are the colour of chestnuts. The carefully-restored carriage barn has three genuinely luxurious suites. The Grahams set a fine example to newer inns striving to achieve a comfortable, low-key and relaxed ambience.

∽

NEARBY beaches, water-sports, cycling; antique shops.
LOCATION in residential area; car parking
FOOD breakfast
PRICE rooms $$ with breakfast
ROOMS 9; all have bath or shower, air-conditioning
FACILITIES dining room, sitting room; terrace, garden
SMOKING no
CREDIT CARDS AE, DC, MC, V
CHILDREN over 10
DISABLED not suitable
CLOSED never
PROPRIETORS Gerrie and Milt Graham

VERMONT

WEST MOUNTAIN INN
~ COUNTRY INN ~

River Road, off Route 313, Arlington, VT 05250
TEL (802) 3756516
E-MAIL info@westmountaininn.com WEBSITE www.westmountaininn.com

YOU MAY BE SURPRISED to see a llama on the sign at the end of the driveway: the Carlsons breed these South American animals but everything else about this spacious former farmhouse is typically Vermont. Set into the hillside and surrounded by extensive grounds, views are over the Battenkill, the famous fly-fishing stream. In the autumn, chrysanthemums mirror the fall foliage, while in winter, cross-country skis stand ready by the front door.

Bedrooms are named after personalities who spent time in the area. The grand Rockwell Kent Suite, 'half-library, half-living room', is big enough for families, and children enjoy clambering up the ladder to sleep in the loft over the bathroom. Works by local artists on the walls plus antiques and cheerful, printed fabrics add up to a look that is 'comfortable and country'.

The Carlsons also grow their own African violets and put one in each bedroom for guests to take home. Some say they have a 'peace and love' philosophy, but this is not off-putting. The atmosphere is genuinely friendly. Although most guests take the dinner, bed and breakfast plan, some readers have been disappointed by the food. More reports, please.

~

NEARBY fly-fishing; cross-country skiing; Bennington museums.
LOCATION near Arlington; car parking
FOOD breakfast, dinner
PRICE rooms $$-$$$ with breakfast
ROOMS 12 double; 3 suites; all have bath or shower
FACILITIES 2 dining rooms, 2 sitting rooms, bar; garden
SMOKING no
CREDIT CARDS AE, MC, V
CHILDREN welcome
DISABLED 1 room
CLOSED never
PROPRIETORS the Carlson family

VERMONT

BARNARD

TWIN FARMS

~ LUXURY RESORT ~

Barnard, VT 05031
TEL (802) 2349999; (800) 8946327 FAX (802) 234 9990
WEBSITE www.twinfarms.com

THE PHILOSOPHY IS SIMPLE: charge a huge sum of money but make everything inclusive so guests can play at being a house-guest in a millionaire's country retreat. Room prices start at $900 but can be twice that. This ambitious project opened in 1993, making much of the Sinclair Lewis connection. The Nobel Prize-winning author (Babbitt, Elmer Gantry) lived in this secluded valley farmhouse with his wife, Dorothy, in the 1930s. Parties for the literati and glitterati were held in the Barn; today, guests have drinks here before dinner. Red's Room (Sinclair's nickname) is one of only four bedrooms in the main home. Dorothy's Room has a Russian theme, with fine water-colours.

There are also cottages: the Studio has an easel, paint splashes on the floor and a Frank Stella above the fireplace. The Treehouse is high above the ground on stilts. Furnishings combine modern art, fine antiques, and natural wood and stone. Fishermen on the lake or skiers on the inn's slope can have a picnic lunch laid out; evenings are dinner parties hosted by the British managers. Talented chef Neil Wigglesworth was at The Point, NY. Fans insist that this is a once-in-a-lifetime, sybaritic experience.

~

NEARBY Woodstock, Billings Farm Museum, Quechee glass mill.
LOCATION on estate; car parking
FOOD breakfast, lunch, dinner
PRICE rooms from $$$$
ROOMS 15; all have bath or shower, air-conditioning, phone, TV, radio, minibar, hairdrier
FACILITIES dining room, sitting room, bar, sauna
SMOKING no
CREDIT CARDS AE, MC, V
CHILDREN over 18
DISABLED not suitable
CLOSED April
MANAGER Michael Beardsley

VERMONT

BRANDON

LILAC INN
~ TOWN MANSION ~

53 Park Street, Brandon, VT 05733
TEL (802) 2475463 FAX (802) 2475499
E-MAIL lilac@sover.net WEBSITE www.lilacinn.com

BRANDON ITSELF may not be the prettiest Vermont village but Park Street, lined with mature maples, is one of New England's handsomest streets. The Lilac Inn comes as a surprise. Instead of the usual Colonial and Federal-style inns, this is a Greek Revival mansion, built as a summer home in 1909 for financier Albert Farr. It was restored by architect Melanie Shane and her husband, Michael. In the summer of 2001, a Connecticut couple, Doug and Shelly Sawyer, took over the inn.

They have made no changes to the decoration, so the bedrooms on the north side still have plenty of yellows to keep them looking cheery in the winter months. Bedroom number 7 has a honey-coloured pine four-poster bed; number 6 has a custom-built oak four poster canopy bed. Most popular room? That has to be Room 8, Kimble's Room, dedicated to Brandon's most famous asset, folk artist Warren Kimble. Folksy stars and stripes flags adorn the walls. The bathrooms are elegant, with luxurious towels and first-class lighting. The inn is hugely popular for weddings, thanks to the grand ballroom and gallery, complete with chandeliers.

~

NEARBY fishing, golf, hiking; cross-country skiing.
LOCATION on avenue; car parking
FOOD breakfast
PRICE rooms $$-$$$$ with breakfast
ROOMS 9; all have bath or shower, air-conditioning, phone, TV
FACILITIES dining room, 2 sitting rooms; terrace, garden
SMOKING no
CREDIT CARDS AE, MC, V
CHILDREN not suitable
DISABLED not suitable
CLOSED never
PROPRIETORS the Sawyers

VERMONT

CASPIAN LAKE

HIGHLAND LODGE

～ RURAL RETREAT ～

Caspian Lake, Greensboro, VT 05841
TEL (802) 5332647 FAX (802) 5337494
E-MAIL highland.lodge@verizon.net WEBSITE www.highlandlodge.com

VERMONT'S NORTHEAST KINGDOM is a landscape of endless woods, calm lakes and pretty villages. Less than an hour north of Montpelier, the state capital, the 150-year-old inn is a sophisticated retreat overlooking a private beach on Caspian Lake. Readers commend the Queen Anne porch with its rocking chairs, the elegant Victorian-style bedrooms, the quality of the food and the 'far from the madding crowds' peace. But most of all, they write about the larger-than-life innkeeper, David Smith and his family. "Their enthusiasm and attention to detail are what make the difference," according to one regular. For those who want to recharge batteries, the library really does provide a wealth of classics. Puzzles old and new are set near the log-burning fireplace. As well as morning activities in the summer and exploring the woods, youngsters have their own playroom with table tennis. For the active, the 30 miles of cross-country ski trails are well known and well groomed. For extra privacy, book into one of the 11 cottages, many with lake views. Included in rates are a hearty breakfast and imaginative dinners, with the option of lunch or a packed picnic.

～

NEARBY craft studios, Cabot Creamery; golf, fishing.
LOCATION deep in country; car parking
FOOD breakfast, lunch, dinner
PRICE rooms $$ with breakfast, dinner
ROOMS 21 double; all have bath or shower
FACILITIES restaurant, sitting rooms; outdoor sports
SMOKING no
CREDIT CARDS MC, V
CHILDREN welcome
DISABLED not suitable
CLOSED never
PROPRIETORS Smith family

VERMONT

CHITTENDEN

FOX CREEK INN
~ RURAL RETREAT ~

Chittenden Dam Road, Chittenden, VT 05737
TEL (802) 4836213; (800) 7070017
E-MAIL ttinn@sover.net WEBSITE www.tuliptreeinn.com

FANS OF THE TULIP TREE INN can breathe easily ... the name has changed but the peace and quiet remain. Follow directions carefully along empty back roads to find a green and white house that matches the pine and birches in the snowy landscape.

The Volz family arrived from Manhattan in December 2000. No wonder Alex smiles when anyone questions the sanity of leaving banking and the civilised world: "This is civilisation." Most guests take the dinner, bed and breakfast plan, since Ann has a growing reputation for her dinner party food. Breakfast might include cinnamon swirl French toast, or blueberry pancakes. Dinner, taken at individual tables unless guests want to push the tables together, might feature crab cakes, duck with a brandy and ginger sauce. The inn's new name is an excuse for the Volz's to show off 30 years of collecting all things foxy, from statues to pictures. They even named their stretch of the brook that burbles through the property 'Fox Creek'. Expect pretty, rustic fabrics with firm modern beds. No wonder readers describe this as 'backwoods luxury'. Ski at Killington in winter; hike and bike in summer. More reports, please.

~

NEARBY woods and more woods.
LOCATION on country road; car parking
FOOD breakfast, dinner
PRICE DB&B from $$-$$$$
ROOMS 9; all have bath or shower
FACILITIES dining room, sitting room, bar; garden
SMOKING no
CREDIT CARDS MC, V
CHILDREN not suitable
DISABLED not suitable
CLOSED April, early May; Nov
PROPRIETORS Ann and Alex Volz

VERMONT

DORSET

BARROWS HOUSE

~ VILLAGE INN ~

Dorset, VT 05251
TEL (802) 8674455; (800) 6391620 FAX (802) 8670132
E-MAIL innkeepers@barrowshouse.com WEBSITE www.barrowshouse.com

WITH A GREEN and a church, a summer theatre and a history dating back to before the American Revolution, Dorset is the epitome of a Vermont village. Right at the heart is the Barrows House, named for the first innkeepers, Theresa and Experience Barrows, who opened to the public in 1900. 'Homey and even a little cluttered' was our first reaction to the country furnishings, embellished with lots of lace and dried flowers. The low ceiling in the dining room makes it feel rather cramped, though this is offset by walls of windows at either end. Menus include Maine crabcakes, duck in a Grand Marnier sauce, salmon in a hazelnut mustard crust and Oreo-crusted white chocolate chip brownies.

The real advantage here is the variety of accommodation, with seven more buildings in the extensive grounds. Couples wanting seclusion like the suite with a working fireplace; families can spread out in the Carriage House or the Truffle House. There is more to do than at many inns: play tennis or croquet, swim or borrow a bicycle. In winter, ski cross-country on local trails or downhill at nearby Bromley and Stratton Mountains. The McGinnis family took over in 1993.

~

NEARBY fishing, canoeing, shopping in Manchester.
LOCATION in village; car parking
FOOD breakfast, dinner
PRICE rooms $$-$$$$ with breakfast
ROOMS 28 double; all have bath or shower; some have air-conditioning, TV
FACILITIES dining room, sitting room; garden, swimming pool
SMOKING restricted
CREDIT CARDS AE, MC, V
CHILDREN welcome
DISABLED 1 room
CLOSED never
PROPRIETORS Linda and Jim McGinnis

VERMONT

DORSET

DORSET INN

~ COLONIAL INN ~

Church Street, Dorset, VT 05251
TEL (802) 8675500 FAX (802) 8675542
E-MAIL info@dorsetinn.com WEBSITE www.dorsetinn.com

WE ARE HAPPY to break the rules for this inn which, with 31 rooms, is well over our limit. Standing right on the green in one of the state's most photogenic villages, the Dorset Inn has dispensed hospitality for 200 years. Climb onto a stool at the big wooden bar in the tavern and order an Otter Creek Stovepipe Porter from the local brewery. In the dining room, the look is 'fox and hounds' with dark green walls, sporting prints and a display of pewter. Chef Sissy Hicks, a protégée of restaurateur Joe Allen, is known for her modern American cuisine: smoked-seafood salad, apple-smoked barbecue chicken, or more traditional fare such as calves liver with onion and bacon.

With several sitting rooms offering plenty of quiet corners for reading or chatting, there is none of the enforced sociability of some small inns. Bedrooms have fresh colour schemes. Like many readers, we liked number 28, with a chest at the foot of the four-poster bed, and views over the village green. Tall guests find the bedrooms under the eaves a bit cramped; others think they are cosy. There are some single rooms, and to complete the rural idyll, there are no telephones or TVs in the rooms.

~

NEARBY summer theatre; Manchester shopping; golf.
LOCATION in village; car parking
FOOD breakfast, lunch, dinner
PRICE rooms $-$$$ including breakfast
ROOMS 31; all have bath or shower
FACILITIES dining room, 3 sitting rooms, bar
SMOKING no
CREDIT CARDS AE, MC, V
CHILDREN over 10
DISABLED restaurant only
CLOSED never
PROPRIETOR Sissy Hicks

VERMONT

EAST MIDDLEBURY

WAYBURY INN

~ COACHING INN ~

Route 125, East Middlebury, VT 05740
TEL (802) 3884015; (800) 3481810
E-MAIL thefolks@wayburyinn.com WEBSITE www.wayburyinn.com

STAGE COACHES would rattle in here to change horses on their way to Boston. That was back in 1810. East Middlebury is far less important today, but the Waybury Inn does have a more recent claim to fame. The exterior was used in the popular Bob Newhart television series, posing as the 'Stratford Inn'. Some memorabilia are left over, such as old sleds, rocking chairs and benches on the front porch.

In 1999, the Suttons, veterans of the hospitality trade, arrived and gave the inn a well-needed facelift, from bedrooms and bathrooms right through to the famous pub, with its moose head over the fireplace. This now looks more like an Airondacks fishing lodge, while the Coach Room and Club Room serve up much better fare than before. As for bedrooms, the most sought after is number 9, called the Robert Frost room, in recognition of the poet who used to eat here regularly. More recently, this room has found fame for its box full of letters, left by couples eager to share their romantic interludes with subsequent guests. We prefer room number 10, on the corner with large windows, with its dark green paint and four poster bed.

~

NEARBY Cross-country, downhill skiing; Middlebury Cottage.
LOCATION in town; car parking
FOOD rooms $-$$ with breakfast
PRICE dinner
ROOMS 15 double; all have bath or shower
FACILITIES dining room, 2 sitting rooms, bar; garden
SMOKING no
CREDIT CARDS AE, MC, V
CHILDREN welcome
DISABLED not suitable
CLOSED 1 week Nov
PROPRIETORS Tracy and Joe Sutton

VERMONT

GOSHEN

BLUEBERRY HILL INN

~ COUNTRY INN ~

Goshen, VT 05733
TEL (802) 2476735; (800) 4480707 FAX (802) 2473983
E-MAIL info2@blueberryhillinn.com WEBSITE www.blueberryhillinn.com

DEEP IN THE MIDDLE of nowhere stands this farmhouse, built by loggers in 1813. Surrounded by the Green Mountain National Forest, this delightful inn appeals to hikers and cross-country skiers, with 40 miles of trails. Rent equipment at the ski centre, which also has snowshoes. Of course, you can just relax, read and do nothing at all. The owner, Tony Clarke, is British but grew up in France. He compares his inn to a French auberge and food is definitely a feature here. At the end of the day, guests congregate for drinks, wine and cheese, before a meal that could include mousseline of scallops, roast duck with ginger and strawberry roulade. It is served family-style, at long tables that encourage conversation, often lasting long into the evening. In the morning, breakfasts are equally fulsome and a speciality is pancakes with blueberries, picket outside the inn. The bedrooms, attractive and comfortable rather than designer-decorated, are in the main house, the Greenhouse and a modern wing. There is a sauna, spring fed pond for swimming, flower and herb garden and lawns for children, or grown-ups to run around. Remember, however, to bring your own wine.

~

NEARBY Lake Champlain Maritime Center, Shelburne Museum.
LOCATION in national forest; car parking
FOOD breakfast, lunch, dinner
PRICE $$$-$$$$, with breakfast, dinner
ROOMS 12 double; all have bath or shower
FACILITIES dining room, 3 sitting rooms, sauna; garden
SMOKING no
CREDIT CARDS MC, V
CHILDREN welcome
DISABLED 1 room
CLOSED sometimes April
PROPRIETOR Tony Clarke

VERMONT

GRAFTON

INN AT WOOD CHUCK HILL FARM

~ RURAL INN ~

Middletown Road, Grafton VT 0514756
TEL (802) 8432398
E-MAIL info@woodchuckhill.com WEBSITE www.woodchuckhill.com

THIS 18THC HOUSE is one of Grafton's oldest and has been the Gabriel family home for three generations. Mark and his wife, Marilyn, took over from his parents who had run the place for 30 years. A fount of local history, he may look the 'conservative country gentleman' but has an understated sense of humour and wears trendy wire-rimmed spectacles.

Ten minutes' drive from the village, the inn stands at the top of a long, steep, dirt road. Views here are truly spectacular: up to 120 km (75 miles) from the porch or the West Room on the top floor, right across to the mountains of New Hampshire. Guests can ramble in the fields and meadows in all directions, and even swim in the pond after a sauna. Most rooms are furnished with country antiques, but the converted Barn has a more contemporary feel with its post and beam construction and the Studio is a modern wood and glass cabin. The Gabriels never advertise, preferring word of mouth recommendation. This is ideal for that elusive vacation, deep in the country. "Even when the inn was full at the height of the foliage season," one reader tells us, "It was still remote and peaceful."

~

NEARBY Grafton; tennis, antique shops
LOCATION off beaten track; car parking
FOOD breakfast
PRICE rooms $$ with breakfast
ROOMS 6 double, 5 suites; all have bath or shower
FACILITIES dining room, sitting room, sauna
SMOKING no
CREDIT CARDS AE, MC, V
CHILDREN welcome
DISABLED not suitable
CLOSED never
PROPRIETORS Mark and Marilyn Gabriel

VERMONT

KILLINGTON

VERMONT INN

~ COUNTRY INN ~

Route 4, Killington, VT 05751
TEL (802) 7750708; (800) 5417795
E-MAIL relax@vermontinn.com WEBSITE www.vermontinn.com

EXPOSED BEAMS, country prints, traditional furniture and brass beds add up to an informal and uncluttered style. The 1840-built house had long been an inn before the Smiths took over in 1996. Although they have enlarged many bedrooms and added several fireplaces, they have been careful to maintain the old-fashioned atmosphere that many expect in a New England inn.

Although some guests merely read or listen to classical music by the wood stove, many are sporty types. In summer, they keep active on the tennis courts and in the swimming-pool, or go cycling or hiking. In winter, they ski downhill at Pico and Killington or cross-country at nearby centres with prepared trails. Afterwards, they have a choice of sauna or hot tub.

This is a larger inn than many, with 18 bedrooms varying in size and colour schemes; some have views of Mount Pico. Favourites include number 1, Grandmother's room and number 15, with its mountain views. Best of all, chef Stephen Hatch is still here after 15 years, preparing his ever-popular French toast at breakfast and stuffed veal dish for dinner. Our inspector recommends the inn for families or anyone on a budget.

~

NEARBY winter sports; canoeing, golf, horse-riding.
LOCATION above Rte 4; ample car parking
FOOD breakfast, dinner
PRICE room $-$$ with breakfast
ROOMS 18 double; most have bath or shower
FACILITIES 2 dining rooms, 2 sitting rooms, bar, sauna, games room; garden, swimming-pool, tennis courts **SMOKING** no
CREDIT CARDS AE, MC, V
CHILDREN over 6
DISABLED 1 bedroom
CLOSED never
PROPRIETORS Megan and Gary Smith

VERMONT

MANCHESTER CENTER

MANCHESTER HIGHLANDS INN

~ BED-AND-BREAKFAST INN ~

Highland Avenue, Manchester Centre, VT 05255
TEL (802) 3624565; (800) 7434565
E-MAIL innkeeper@hihglandsinn.com WEBSITE www.highlandsinn.com

MANCHESTER is one of those small New England towns that manages to offer the best of both worlds, year-round. As well as the glories of the countryside, with downhill skiing and fly-fishing, there is the magnet of the Manchester Designer Outlets for shopping. Confirmation that our readers know a good inn when they stay at one came in 2001 when the Eichorns were named 'Innkeepers of the Year': quite an achievement in Vermont. Receiving much of the praise is another member of the family, Humphrey the cat.

Away from the bustle on a quiet side street, the Victorian inn has everything for the lazy: lawn chairs, hammocks, plus croquet for the more energetic. Don't miss watching the sun set over Mount Equinox from a rocker on the porch. A recent facelift ensured that there are down comforters and feather beds in all bedrooms. In the main house, the Turret Room is requested for its mountain view, while the Lake Champlain Room in the Carriage House is booked for its fireplace. Also in demand are recipes for the lemon soufflé pancakes at breakfast and freshly baked cakes for afternoon tea.

~

NEARBY Mount Equinox, Hildene, shopping; golf, fishing, skiing.
LOCATION in town; car parking
FOOD breakfast
PRICE rooms $$ with breakfast
ROOMS 15 double; all have bath or shower
FACILITIES sitting room; outdoor sports
SMOKING no
CREDIT CARDS MC, V
CHILDREN welcome
DISABLED not suitable
CLOSED never
PROPRIETORS Eichorn family

VERMONT

MANCHESTER VILLAGE

1811 HOUSE

~ BED AND-BREAKFAST INN ~

Manchester Village, VT 05254
TEL (802) 3621811; (800) 4321811
E-MAIL info@1811house.com WEBSITE www.1811house.com

BRUCE DUFF is the sort of genial host who likes to sell the area and its history. The grand summer homes in this mountain village date from the 19th century and include Hildene, the home of President Abraham Lincoln's son. His grand-daughter lived for a while in this building that dates back to 1775 but is named for the date it opened to guests as an inn. The small entry hall leads right into the 'Pub', a very British-style bar, with dark wood, darts and polished brasses. These, along with the single malt whiskies, reflect the family's Scottish ancestry, as do the decorative tartans and the MacDuff coat of arms in the library.

The informality of the Duffs softens the formality of the furniture, giving a pleasant atmosphere. Bedrooms are named for people associated with the house, such as the Henry and Ethel Robinson room, whose private porch has views of the extensive gardens, nearby golf course and the Green Mountains. Many have four-poster beds set off by vibrant colour schemes of gold and green or red and navy blue. On the weekend, the so-called English breakfast consists of scones as well as the usual eggs, bacon and tomato.

~

NEARBY outlet shopping; golf, fishing.
LOCATION in Village; car parking
FOOD breakfast, lunch, dinner
PRICE rooms $$-$$$ with breakfast
ROOMS 13 double; 1 suite; all have bath or shower, air-conditioning
FACILITIES dining room, 2 sitting rooms, bar; garden
SMOKING no
CREDIT CARDS AE, MC, V
CHILDREN over 16
DISABLED not suitable
CLOSED never
PROPRIETORS Bruce and Marnie Duff, Cathy and Jorge Veleta

VERMONT

MANCHESTER VILLAGE

RELUCTANT PANTHER

~ VICTORIAN HOUSE ~

West Road, Manchester Village, VT 05254
TEL (802) 3622568; (800) 8222331 FAX (802) 3622586
E-MAIL stay@reluctantpanther.com WEBSITE www.reluctanpanther.com

THE OUTSIDE of this former merchant's home, dating from 1850, gives a clue to the owner's taste: 'blackberry sorbet' with yellow shutters. Inside, the skilful combinations of fabrics and colours look like the work of an experienced decorator. In fact, they are the choice of Peruvian Maye Bachofen, whose husband, Robert, is a Swiss-trained hotelier with plenty of international experience.

Their style is more formal than many country inns, with crystal glasses and white tablecloths in the restaurant. This has an enormous stone fireplace, balanced by lush plants that thrive by a conservatory-like glass wall. Menus read more like a city restaurant than a rural inn: steamed mussels with saffron-thyme sauce, duck with cassis reduction, Swiss walnut torte with honey and allspice. The Bachofens are as proud of their American and French wines as they are of their collection of Port.

Old pewter door locks are a striking feature of the bedrooms, which continue the high level of comfort. Some have working fireplaces, whirlpool baths and four-poster beds. Bathrooms are modern, with abundant towels. 'Memorable and well-run.'

~

NEARBY shopping; golf, fishing; winter sports.
LOCATION on side street; car parking
FOOD breakfast, dinner
PRICE rooms $$-$$$$ with breakfast
ROOMS 12 double, 4 suites; all have bath or shower, air-conditioning, phone, TV
FACILITIES 2 dining rooms, sitting room, bar; terrace
SMOKING no
CREDIT CARDS AE, MC, V
CHILDREN over 14
DISABLED not suitable
CLOSED never
PROPRIETORS Robert and Maye Bachofen

VERMONT

MENDON

RED CLOVER INN

~ COUNTRY INN ~

Woodward Road, Mendon, VT 05701
TEL (802) 7752290; (800) 7520571 FAX (802) 7730594
E-MAIL innkeepers@redcloverinn.com WEBSITE www.redcloverinn.com

UNITED STATES ARMY GENERAL John Woodward knew what he was doing when he built this summer home in the shallow of Mount Pico. That was in the 1840s; now, although a busy main road passes nearby, the rural peace remains undisturbed. With its classic New England red barn, the look is more 'farm' than 'inn'. Since taking over early in 2001, the Streleckis, who 'left Texas to get away from the heat', have changed little.

So in the bedrooms, colourful patchwork quilts stand out against the plain cream, brown or red paintwork, while ruffled white curtains frame vistas of fields and trees. Readers commend Country Casual, with its cathedral ceiling, snug Mountain Retreat with its exposed beams and Garden Gables, with its mountain views. All have luxurious bathrooms. The spacious sitting room has high-back armchairs and big sofas under the exposed beams of the wood ceiling. Dinner menus are adventurous: Maine scallop and crab cakes, lobster ravioli with orange beurre blanc, horseradish crusted salmon. Guests do not have to go far for excersise: cross-country ski trails pass the door and there is a swimming-pool in the garden.

~

NEARBY Killington and Pico ski areas; hiking, summer theatre.
LOCATION off Rte 4; car parking
FOOD breakfast, dinner
PRICE rooms $$-$$$ with breakfast
ROOMS 14 double; all have bath or shower
FACILITIES 3 dining rooms, sitting room, bar; garden
SMOKING no
CREDIT CARDS MC, V
CHILDREN over 8
DISABLED not suitable
CLOSED never
PROPRIETORS Mary and Dave Strelecki, Melinda Davis

VERMONT

MIDDLEBURY

SWIFT HOUSE INN

~ HISTORIC INN ~

25 Stewart Lane, Middlebury, VT 05753
TEL (802) 3889925 FAX (802) 3889927
E-MAIL shi@together.net WEBSITE www.swifthouseinn.com

FROM THE OUTSIDE, this looks like a posh private house in what is a posh small town, complete with a posh small college. There is a minimum of signs and advertising for this inn, part of which dates from 1812.

The Federal style is maintained in the lobby and living room, where not a magazine or puzzle is out of place. Voices are automatically lowered in this elegant, refined atmosphere, best-suited to adults, not families with children. Dinner is no longer served in the cherry-panelled dining room, but breakfast offerings range from the usual muffins to Vermont apple cider, quiches, smoked salmon and smoked trout. The bedrooms reflect the hand of a decorator. The large Swift Room has a whirlpool tub, terry-cloth bathrobes and a terrace; the Governor's Room, painted in Wedgewood blue and cream, also boasts a whirlpool bath. There are two other separate buildings: the Carriage House and the Gatehouse.

In 1996, Karla Nelson-Lovra joined her father John at an inn that is undeniably attractive and professionally-run…but just a little stuffy.

~

NEARBY Middlebury and its college; winter sports.
LOCATION in side street; car parking
FOOD breakfast
PRICE rooms $-$$$ with breakfast
ROOMS 21 double; all have bath or shower, air-conditioning, phone; some have TV
FACILITIES 2 dining rooms, 3 sitting rooms, bar, sauna; terrace, garden
SMOKING restricted
CREDIT CARDS AE, DC, MC, V
CHILDREN not suitable
DISABLED 1 room
CLOSED never
INNKEEPER Karla Nelson-Loura

VERMONT

NEWFANE

FOUR COLUMNS INN

~ HOTEL-RESTAURANT ~

PO Box 278, Newfane, VT 05345
TEL (802) 3657713
E-MAIL innkeeper@fourcolumnsinn.com WEBSITE www.fourcolumnsinn.com

NEWFANE IS NOT particularly convenient for skiing or shopping, but tourists flock here to photograph the village green, with its old-fashioned courthouse, church, general store and houses. They also come to the two well-known inns. At the west end of the green, the Four Columns looks truly impressive, its Greek Revival columns built over 150 years ago by General Pardon Kimball to remind his wife of her southern home.

The herb garden by the front door is a clue that food is of major importance here and Greg Parks' cooking has won the inn renown. Grilled sweetbreads and lobster raviolette for starters, main courses of chicken with Tuscan sausage or grilled duck breast with baked duck leg: these are crossovers from classic European to innovative North American cuisine. The restaurant is in a converted barn which also has some bedrooms, others are in the main house and the cottage by the pond where ice-skating is possible in winter. Pam and Gorty Baldwin, who took over in 1999, have made the bedrooms more luxurious than ever, with vast beds, glamorous bathrooms, cathedral ceilings and thick Oriental carpets. "One of the most romantic inns ever," according to one reader.

~

NEARBY covered bridges; hiking, cycling.
LOCATION on village green; car parking
FOOD breakfast, dinner
PRICE rooms $$-$$$$ with breakfast
ROOMS 15 double; all have bath or shower
FACILITIES dining room, 2 sitting rooms, bar; terrace, garden, swimming pool
SMOKING no
CREDIT CARDS AE, MC, V
CHILDREN over 10
DISABLED not suitable, lift/elevator
CLOSED never
PROPRIETORS Pam and Gorty Baldwin

VERMONT

NEWFANE

OLD NEWFANE INN

~ OLD COACHING INN ~

Court Street, Newfane, VT 05345
TEL (802) 3654427; (800) 7844427
WEBSITE www.oldnewfaneinn.com

THE VILLAGE OF NEWFANE was originally 2 miles (3 km) away on Newfane Hill but was moved lock, stock and barrel to its present site by sleigh in 1825. Among the buildings taken apart and rebuilt was the Old Newfane Inn, which stands right on the green. A classic coaching stop, its long side faces the common with a rambling, ancient grape vine growing the length of the building. A porch runs the length as well, with white and green chairs and rockers. Inside, a corner is devoted to the reception area where walls are hung with a mass of framed articles about the inn.

In the long dining room, a heavy-timbered ceiling, brick fireplace wall and pewter plates on the tables give a real feel of the 18thC Colonial era. German-born but Swiss-trained Eric Weindl has been here some 30 years but the service as well as the cooking remain strictly European: veal goulash is served with spätzle, there are snails, Burgundian-style, Châteaubriand and an impressive list of wines.

The bedrooms are elegant and filled with above-average antiques. The atmosphere is genteel and somewhat formal; rather like the other inn in the village, this is a 'special occasion' place.

~

NEARBY covered bridges; hiking, cycling.
LOCATION on the green; car parking
FOOD breakfast, dinner
PRICE rooms $$ with breakfast
ROOMS 10 double, all have bath or shower
FACILITIES dining room, sitting room, bar
SMOKING no
CREDIT CARDS MC, V
CHILDREN over 10
DISABLED not suitable
CLOSED April to mid-May; Nov to mid-Dec; restaurant only, Mon
PROPRIETORS Eric and Gundy Weindl

VERMONT

SIMONSVILLE

ROWELL'S INN
∽ COACHING INN ∽

RFD1, Box 2670, Simonsville, Chester, VT 05143
TEL (802) 8753658; (800) 7280842 FAX (802) 8753680
E-MAIL innkeeper@rowellsinn.com WEBSITE www.rowellsinn.com

THE DISTINCTIVE THREE-STOREYED porches topped by a Bennington flag face a bend on a country road: blink and you could miss it. What started out as a stagecoach halt in the early 19thC claims to be the oldest real hotel in the state and is on the National Register of Historic Places. Innkeepers Michael Brengolini and Susan McNulty have taken over from Beth and Lee Davis, whose British pub at the rear is still an atmospheric haunt for a beer and a chat. The rooms have been refreshed, with historic names such as Miss Caitlin and Master William. For extra comfort, Major Simons and F A Rowell both offer room to spread out to read a book. Both have grand beds: one an enamel and brass canopy, the other an impressive double pine cone poster.

With advance warning, guests can enjoy hearty dinner party fare with a New England accent: Vermont Cheddar pie, pork with applesauce, fudge caramel pecan pie. This is not for people who want fancy food or opulent furnishings. In chilly weather, many laze around in the front parlour, the glassed-in sun porch at the rear, or the tavern. In fall and summer, they are out hiking and exploring Southern Vermont. ∽

NEARBY Weston; Bromley and Magic Mountain ski areas.
LOCATION on country road; car parking
FOOD breakfast, dinner
PRICE $-$$$
ROOMS 7 double; all have bath or shower
FACILITIES dining room, 2 sitting rooms, bar; terrace, garden
SMOKING no
CREDIT CARDS AE, MC, V
CHILDREN over 12
DISABLED not suitable
CLOSED sometimes April
PROPRIETORS Michael Brengolini & Susan McNulty

VERMONT

INN AT THE ROUND BARN FARM

~ LUXURY BED-AND-BREAKFAST ~

RR1, Box 247, East Warren Road, Waitsfield, VT 05673
TEL (802) 4962276 FAX (802) 4968832
E-MAIL info@innattheroundbarn.com WEBSITE www.innattheroundbarn.com

ROUND BARNS were supposedly built by the Shakers 'because the devil can't catch you in a corner'. Today, one of Vermont's few remaining circular dairy barns has been carefully restored by Jack and Doreen Simko. Built in 1910, it is now used for conferences and weddings. Set in a hillside, the inn next door is unashamedly luxurious but somehow it all works because the honey-coloured pine floors are original, the canopy beds are old and the glitzy bathrooms overlook woods and meadows.

The Simkos renovated the buildings themselves. Patterned fabrics balance plain walls, oriental carpets lie on wood floors and antiques are handsome but not museum pieces. There are fireplaces and, in the Sherman Room, the exposed timbers of the high, steeply-angled roof. Bathrooms are among the best we have seen, with huge towels, steam showers, whirlpool tubs and views over the hillside. The Simkos had no hotel training but were in the flower business, hence the profuse arrangements.

Their daughter, Anne Marie, is now in charge of the inn, as well as her famous breakfasts: perhaps pancakes with raspberry maple syrup. She also runs cookery courses.

~

NEARBY skiing at Sugarbush, Sugarbush North, Mad River Glen.
LOCATION on quiet road; car parking
FOOD breakfast
PRICE rooms $-$$$ with breakfast
ROOMS 12 double; all have bath or shower; some air-conditioning
FACILITIES dining room, 2 sitting rooms, indoor swimming pool; garden
SMOKING no
CREDIT CARDS AE, MC, V
CHILDREN over 15
DISABLED not suitable
CLOSED never
INNKEEPER Anne Marie DeFreest

VERMONT

WEST DOVER

DEERHILL INN

~ COUNTRY INN ~

Valley View Road, PO Box 136, West Dover, VT 05356
TEL (802) 4643100; (800) 9933379 FAX (802) 4645474
E-MAIL deerhill@sover.net WEBSITE www.deerhill.com

WHAT SETS THIS inn apart is the high-quality cooking of chef/owner Michael Anelli. Back in 1995, he and his wife, Linda, who runs the front of the house, took over from the Ritchies, a British couple. Their legacy is the English garden. In the heart of southern Vermont's ski areas, with a host of pretty villages to explore in summer and fall, this is an ideal base.

Breakfasts follow tradition: blueberry pancakes, slathered with Vermont maple syrup, freshly-baked muffins. In the evening, the tempo changes, with flickering candles and fresh flowers. To complement this romantic setting, Chef Michael features local produce such as Vermont pheasant, trout and maple-glazed chicken, alongside more exotic Cajun-style shrimp. His ice cream brownie cake is irresistible. The bedrooms are also romantic, decorated with a full palette of colours, from bright green walls to floral wallpapers, with a scattering of antiques, paintings and cushions.

Set on a hill with a fine view over the village of West Dorset, the swimming-pool and tennis court are a definite bonus in summer. Ski at Mount Snow and Haystacks in winter.

~

NEARBY skiing; golf, fishing, hiking; Marlboro Music Festival.
LOCATION in country; car parking
FOOD breakfast, dinner
PRICE rooms $-$$$ with breakfast
ROOMS 15 double; all have bath or shower
FACILITIES dining room, sitting room; garden, swimming-pool, tennis court
SMOKING no
CREDIT CARDS AE, MC, V
CHILDREN over 8
DISABLED not suitable
CLOSED 3 weeks Nov; April/May
PROPRIETORS Linda and Michael Anelli

VERMONT

WEST DOVER

INN AT SAWMILL FARM

~ LUXURY HOTEL ~

PO Box 367, Route 100, West Dover, VT 05356
TEL (802) 4648131 FAX (802) 4641130
E-MAIL sawmill@sover.net WEBSITE www.vermontdirect.com/sawmill

THIS IS AN INN OF CONTRASTS. The outside looks like a large converted barn; in the entrance hall, the brick floor, old farm tools and a wrought-iron chandelier are reminders that this was a farm when the Williams family (architect and designer) bought it as a ski home in 1967. Now, however, it is one of the most luxurious inns in the whole state. The atmosphere is 'posh country elegance', with boldly-patterned curtains in the sitting room and museum-quality antiques such as the sideboard in the formal dining room.

Food and wine are part of the overall attraction of this member of the Relais Châteaux group. Chef Brill Williams has 36,000 bottles in the cellar, ranging from reliable house wines to 1969 Burgundies, while his cooking is classically European: French and Italian dishes such as breast of pheasant with a forestiere sauce or scaloppini of veal marsala.

Bedrooms are just as grand, with modern bathrooms and voluminous towels. This is not the place for weary skiers hoping to find a bargain room; the appeal is to well-off weekenders who want to be pampered and might ski at Mt Snow if conditions are perfect.

~

NEARBY winter-sports; golf; cycling; Marlboro Music Festival.
LOCATION in country town; car parking
FOOD breakfast, dinner
PRICE DB&B only from $$$$
ROOMS 20 double; all have bath or shower, phone, TV
FACILITIES 3 dining rooms, 3 sitting rooms, bar; garden, swimming pool, tennis court
SMOKING no
CREDIT CARDS AE, MC, V
CHILDREN over 10
DISABLED not suitable
CLOSED April, May
PROPRIETORS Ione and Rodney Williams, Brill Williams

VERMONT

WEST TOWNSHEND

WINDHAM HILL
~ COUNTRY RETREAT ~

West Townshend, VT 05359
TEL (802) 8744080; (800) 9444080
E-MAIL windham@sover.net WEBSITE www.windhamhill.com

WITH ITS VILLAGE GREEN and covered bridge, Townshend has long been popular with camera-toting visitors. By contrast, the Windham Hill is well away from the crowds, on a rise above the West River Valley. Built in 1823, this rambling farmstead has splendid views over the huge estate of woods and meadows. Thirteen bedrooms are in the main house, eight more in the converted barn. 'This is not a frilly, lacy kind of place,' although there are candles, antique wall-clocks and a Steinway piano that is a focal point of the Wicker Room where guests have pre-dinner drinks.

Each bedroom is different. Tree House looks out into branches from a comfortable window-seat; Kate's Room has a cherry wood bed and two old babies' dresses on the wall as decoration. One bedroom is adapted for disabled guests. In contrast with many inns striving for the 'romantic' image, the ambience here is healthy, even spiritual, and in tune with the rural surroundings. Guests may choose to be at separate tables or the conviviality of dining with others at a large table. Special dishes on an incentive menu include scallops with truffled potatoes and quail with a molasses glaze. Cross-country ski lessons are available.

~

NEARBY cross-country trails, downhill skiing, fishing, hiking.
LOCATION just outside Townshend; car parking
FOOD breakfast, dinner
PRICE DB&B from $$
ROOMS 21 double; all have bath or shower, phone
FACILITIES 2 dining rooms, 2 sitting rooms; garden; cross-country ski school
SMOKING no
CREDIT CARDS AE, MC, V
CHILDREN over 12
DISABLED 1 room
CLOSED never
PROPRIETORS Grigs and Pat Markham

VERMONT

WESTON

INN AT WESTON
~ TOWN INN ~

Route 100, Weston, VT 05161
TEL (802) 8245804 FAX (802) 8243073
E-MAIL info@innweston.com WEBSITE www.innweston.com

WESTON IS A CLASSIC Vermont village with a bandstand on the green, a white church on the hill and a famous village store. In summer, the drama season at the well-known Playhouse is a major attraction; in the fall, crowds come for the famous foliage. But the focal point of village life is this inn. Built as a farmhouse in 1848, but only converted for guests in 1951, the Aldrichs have transformed and upgraded the property since their arrival from New Jersey in 1998. Small rooms have been sacrificed to make larger and much more comfortable rooms, along with better bathrooms. Five rooms are in the main inn, six more in the Coleman House across the street. Newest and most luxurious are the two in the Carriage House. In the deep red, intimate dining room, readers have been quick to praise Chef Max Turner for dishes such as mango lobster Louie and mocha crème brûlée. They also like the breakfast offerings that get away from the usual blueberry pancakes to include Vermont cheese and apple omelettes and smoked salmon eggs Benedict. The Aldrichs love orchids and have built a glasshouse to show off their collection.

~

NEARBY Playhouse, Vermont Country Store.
LOCATION in village; car parking
FOOD breakfast, dinner
PRICE rooms $$-$$$$ with breakfast
ROOMS 13 double; all have bath or shower, phone; some air-conditioning, radio, TV
FACILITIES dining room, 2 sitting rooms, bar
SMOKING no
CREDIT CARDS AE, MC, V
CHILDREN over 14
DISABLED not suitable
CLOSED never
PROPRIETORS Linda and Bob Aldrich

VERMONT

WILMINGTON

TRAIL'S END
～ RURAL INN ～

Smith Road, Wilmington, VT 05363
TEL (802) 4642727; (800) 8592585
E-MAIL trailsnd@together.net WEBSITE www.trailsendvt.com

"IF I WAS GOING to live in a hotel, I figured I may as well live in my own," jokes Kevin Stephens, who gave up travelling the world on computer business to move to this retreat in 1997. Unlike the majority of New England bed-and-breakfasts with their Colonial, Victorian or farmhouse architecture, this was built as a ski lodge in 1956. Standing among pine trees, Trail's End looks like a lodge in one of America's Western states. The interior has a contemporary, country feel with a two-storey stone fireplace in the split-level sitting-room. As for bedrooms, most have stone fireplaces, Kevin's antiques and family heirlooms, cable TV and VCRs (borrow from 100 videos).

In summer, couples come for the outstanding chamber concert festival in nearby Marlboro; they also use the tennis court, outdoor, heated swimming-pool and trout pond. In fall, the attraction is the foliage, while winter snow is plentiful for skiing. But many come and do nothing but read and loaf. If couples do not want to mix, Kevin has a games room with an eight-foot pool table. Breakfasts of traditional eggs, sausages and thick toast are served family-style, at large oak tables.

～

NEARBY Mt Snow, Haystack ski areas; hiking, fishing, cycling.
LOCATION in countryside; car parking
FOOD breakfast
PRICE rooms $$-$$$ with breakfast
ROOMS 13 double; 2 suites; all have bath or shower **FACILITIES** dining room, sitting room; garden, swimming-pool, tennis court, trout pond
SMOKING no
CREDIT CARDS MC, V
CHILDREN welcome
DISABLED not suitable
CLOSED never
PROPRIETOR Kevin Stephens

NEW HAMPSHIRE

BETHLEHEM

ADAIR

∼ LUXURY BED-AND-BREAKFAST ∼

Old Littleton Road, Bethlehem, NH 03574
TEL (603) 4442600; (888) 4412600 FAX (603) 4444823
E-MAIL adair@conriver.net WEBSITE www.adairinn.com

To CALL THIS a country inn is like describing Windsor Castle as a weekend retreat. Set in a huge estate, the landscaping was by Frederick Olmsted, who also designed New York's Central Park and Boston's Emerald Necklace. The house itself was a 1927 wedding gift for the daughter of a Washington lawyer. Presidents, sports heroes and film stars visited regularly until it was converted into a somewhat formal bed-and-breakfast, complete with swimming-pool and tennis court in 1992. Today, the Whitmans, from Chicago, are only the third owners.

The nine bedrooms in the main house are large, each named after one of the mountains in the Presidential Range. All compare with a five star hotel for luxury, with big beds, robes, thick carpets and chocolates. Seven have fireplaces. Jackson Cottage, in the grounds, has two bedrooms. Judy Whitman's breakfasts are elegant and elaborate: home-baked breads, eggs Dijonnais, lemon chiffon pancakes. English-style afternoon teas are another highlight. In the evening, the well-reviewed Tim-Bir Alley restaurant (a separate operation) takes over in the dining-room where non-residents are welcome to book tables.

∼

NEARBY White Mountains, winter sports, golf, fishing.
LOCATION outside village; car parking
FOOD breakfast
PRICE rooms $$-$$$ with breakfast
ROOMS 10; all have bath or shower
FACILITIES dining room, sitting room, bar; garden, swimming-pool, tennis court
SMOKING no
CREDIT CARDS AE, MC, V
CHILDREN not suitable
DISABLED not suitable
CLOSED never
PROPRIETORS Bill and Judy Whitman

NEW HAMPSHIRE

BRETTON WOODS

BRETTON ARMS COUNTRY INN

~ LUXURY COUNTRY INN ~

Route 302, Bretton Woods, NH 03575
TEL (603) 2781000; (800) 2580330 FAX (603) 2788838
E-MAIL brettonarms@mtwashington.com WEBSITE www.mtwashington.com

READERS INSIST that this is an overlooked jewel in the heart of the White Mountains. Everyone has heard about the Mount Washington resort, one of America's grandes dames, with a firm place in history. In 1944, the International Monetary Conference met here and established the World Bank among other fiscal decisions. The Bretton Arms, the small hotel in the grounds of the resort, housed the Secretariat.

After several changes of fortune, the Victorian inn was restored and upgraded in 1986. Now there are all the comforts that city folk demand in the country: a Parlor Lounge with fireplace, an intimate and high-class gourmet restaurant and 34 most comfortable rooms. Regular guests come because they can enjoy the 'small inn experince', while taking advantage of the resort's fine sports facilities, just a short walk away. They can swim, play tennis, ski and, best of all, play golf. In 1915, Scottish golf architect Donald Ross designed what is now an American legend. The only problem with the 6,638-yard, par 71 course is concentrating on your game, with the breathtaking sight of Mount Washington right in front of you.

~

NEARBY White Mountains, Cog Railway; summer, winter sports.
LOCATION on estate; car parking
FOOD breakfast, dinner
PRICE rooms $$-$$$ with breakfast
ROOMS 34; all have bath or shower, TV
FACILITIES dining room, sitting room, bar; sports
SMOKING no
CREDIT CARDS AE, MC, V
CHILDREN over 12
DISABLED not suitable
CLOSED never
MANAGER Eleonore Imrie

NEW HAMPSHIRE

CONWAY

DARBY FIELD INN

⌒ RURAL RETREAT ⌒

Bald Hill, Conway, NH 03818
TEL (603) 4472181; (800) 4264147 FAX (603) 4475726
E-MAIL marc@darbyfield.com WEBSITE www.darbyfield.com

WITH NORTH CONWAY and its frantic shopping so close, the peace and quiet here comes as a relief. The long uphill drive is worth it just for the views, according to our inspector. From the dining room, the mountain ranges roll away to Mount Washington on the horizon. Appropriately, the inn is named after the persistent Irishman who was the first European to scale that peak back in 1642. Maria Donaldson, a massage therapist, who runs the inn with husband Marc, is also an outdoor type, encouraging guests to enjoy the mountain climbing, canoeing or skiing as well as the swimming pool in the well-tended garden,

The inn itself was built in 1860 but has been added to over the years. The usual array of nooks and crannies are stuffed with antiques; a spinning wheel stands next to the fieldstone fireplace. The bedrooms, which seem lighter than most, are all different: number 2, Laura's Room, is large with Victorian furnishings. The suite has been remodelled recently and now has a Jacuzzi, but who needs television when you have a prize-winning view from the window? Food in the restaurant is familiar, reliable, and like a dinner-party menu: rack of lamb, roast duck, French apple pie.

⌒

NEARBY White Mountains; Conway/North Conway shopping.
LOCATION on hilltop; car parking
FOOD breakfast, dinner
PRICE rooms $$ with breakfast
ROOMS 14 double; all have bath or shower
FACILITIES dining room, sitting room; garden, swimming pool
SMOKING restricted
CREDIT CARDS AE, MC, V
CHILDREN over 6
DISABLED not suitable
CLOSED April
PROPRIETORS Marc and Maria Donaldson

NEW HAMPSHIRE

CRAWFORD'S NOTCH/HART'S LOCATION

NOTCHLAND INN

~ MANOR HOUSE ~

Route 302, Hart's Location, NH 03812
TEL (603) 3746131; (800) 8666131 FAX (603) 3746168
E-MAIL notchland@aol.com WEBSITE www.notchlandinn.com

MINUTES FROM Crawford Notch, the state's famous scenic attraction, the gabled 1862 Notchland Inn is an English-style granite manor house, complete with well-tended gardens. From the welcome to the daily weather forecast and the dozens of CDs to borrow, attention to detail is what sets this inn apart. The woodwork gleams, the flowers are fresh, the room decorations are attractive without being fussy. The impressive front parlour was designed by Gustav Stickley, a founder of the Arts and Crafts movement. Rather than TVs and telephones, all 13 rooms have views that readers insist 'are worth the price alone', while the fireplaces make winter visits twice as much fun. Soaking in the outdoor tub as snowflakes fall is another pleasure. Served in a cheerful room with views of ponds and busy bird feeders, breakfast is fresh and appetising. Dinner is a well-priced, slow-paced, five-course affair, with dishes such as a tomato bisque, salmon in a citrus sauce, perfectly-cooked steak and thin pecan tart. We applaud the provision of plastic bags to take home any used soap: a small but sensible eco-touch. We also like the two Bernese Mountain dogs, Abby and Coco.

~

NEARBY White Mountains, winter sports, golf, fishing.
LOCATION in White Mountains; car parking
FOOD breakfast, dinner
PRICE rooms $$$ with breakfast
ROOMS 12; all have bath or shower
FACILITIES dining room, sitting room, bar; garden
SMOKING no
CREDIT CARDS AE, MC, V
CHILDREN over 12
DISABLED not suitable
CLOSED never
INNKEEPERS Les Schoof and Ed Butler; Kath Harris

NEW HAMPSHIRE

FRANCONIA

HORSE AND HOUND

~ RESTAURANT-INN ~

205 Wells Road, Franconia, NH 03580
TEL (603) 8235501; (800) 4505501 FAX (603) 8235501
E-MAIL hound@together.net WEBSITE www.bestinns.net

SINCE 1989, the owners have upgraded this 1830 farmhouse-turned-inn that stands on a quiet country road, well away from Franconia Village. While the exterior is plain, the interior has antiques, paintings and handsome 19thC bronzes. Despite the name of the inn, the only horses and dogs are in the expansive collection of old hunting prints on the walls.

In the broad sitting room, a desk on one side acts as the reception. The dining room has extraordinarily wide pine panels while lushly printed fabric covers the tables, which are covered by glass tops. Bill Steele, the chef, sticks to the sensible, hearty sort of food favoured by hikers and skiers who are regulars: grilled lamb chops and steaks, roast duck and pastas, as well as lighter stir fries. A growing collection of teddy bears is taking over the sitting room and, unusually, (live) pets are welcome. Upstairs, the bedrooms are comfortable without being posh, "though we would put in Jacuzzis if we could afford it". Number 2 has a queen-sized bed so high off the ground that guests really do have to "climb in". This is an engagingly relaxed sort of place, despite the antiques and attractive furnishings.

~

NEARBY Franconia Notch, Cannon Mountain ski area.
LOCATION on country road; car parking
FOOD breakfast, dinner
PRICE rooms $$ with breakfast
ROOMS 10; all have bath or shower
FACILITIES dining room, sitting room
SMOKING restricted
CREDIT CARDS AE, DC, MC, V
CHILDREN welcome
DISABLED not suitable
CLOSED April to mid-May, Oct to Thanksgiving
PROPRIETORS Jim Cantlon, Bill Steele

NEW HAMPSHIRE

GLEN

BERNERHOF INN

～ HOTEL-RESTAURANT ～

Route 302, Glen, NH 03838
TEL (603) 3839132; (800) 5488007
E-MAIL stay@bernerhofinn.com WEBSITE www.bernerhofinn.com

THIS TURN-OF-THE-CENTURY building has been extensively remodelled, providing a distinctive saw-tooth roof line, quickly recognizable from the busy road. The former owners were Swiss and the black bear of Bern remains on the weathervane; the pub of the same name, with more black bears, is a well-known rendezvous and features ski memorabilia from both sides of the Atlantic. Attitash ski resort is two minutes away.

The atmosphere here is more Old World than New, particularly in the restaurant, which really sets the Bernerhof apart. Here, classic European dishes, often based on veal, are served. The Taste of the Mountains Cooking School has been a great success for nearly two decades, emphasising the sophistication of the cooking. As for bedrooms, these vary in everything but quality: number 4 is light and airy with a king-sized brass bed and attractive tiling in the bathroom; number 8 may be small, but has a Jacuzzi plus a mini-television hidden in the armoire; number 7, a suite with a corner dormer window, boasts a sauna and stained-glass panels round the 'Olympic size' Jacuzzi. They are linked with the cheaper Red Apple Inn next door.

NEARBY skiing; Mt Washington Valley, golf, tennis, hiking, fishing.
LOCATION set back from Route 302; car parking
FOOD breakfast, lunch, dinner
PRICE rooms $-$$ with breakfast
ROOMS 7 double; 2 suites; all have bath or shower, phone, TV
FACILITIES 3 dining rooms, sitting room, bar
SMOKING no
CREDIT CARDS AE, MC, V
CHILDREN welcome
DISABLED not suitable
CLOSED never
PROPRIETORS June and George Phillips

NEW HAMPSHIRE

HANCOCK

HANCOCK INN 1789

~ WAYSIDE INN ~

33 Main Street, Hancock, NH 03449
TEL (603) 5253318; (800) 5251789 FAX (603) 5259301
E-MAIL innkeeper@hancockinn.com WEBSITE www.hancockinn.com

THROUGHOUT NEW ENGLAND there are old village inns that have become overly commercial. Happily, this, the oldest in the state, is not one of them. Hancock itself is a quiet place, with a green, bandstand, Norway Pond and some elegant, century-old houses. The inn dates from 1789 and a portrait of its namesake, the bold signatory of the Declaration of Independence, stares down approvingly in the entrance. The building's proportions create a slightly formal air yet, despite being filled with the appropriate antiques, there is a comfort and welcome that makes it appealing. Most bedrooms have the usual four-poster or canopy beds and hooked rugs. The exception is the Rufus Porter or Mural Room, with walls painted by 19thC primitive artist Rufus Porter; stencilling by his friend Moses Eaton is reproduced in number 15, the bedroom next door.

The restaurant serves traditional dishes with an unusual twist: pot roast comes with cranberries, salmon is spiced with coriander and Southern peach pie is accompanied by a raspberry coulis. After 20 years, the popular owners, the Johnstons retired in 2001, and Robert Short took over. More reports, please.

~

NEARBY Mount Monadnock, Peterborough summer theatre.
LOCATION in village; car parking
FOOD breakfast, dinner
PRICE rooms $$ with breakfast
ROOMS 15 double; all have bath or shower, air-conditioning, phone
FACILITIES 2 dining rooms, 3 sitting rooms, bar
SMOKING no
CREDIT CARDS AE, MC, V
CHILDREN over 12
DISABLED 1 room
CLOSED never
PROPRIETOR Robert Short

NEW HAMPSHIRE

HENNIKER

COLBY HILL INN

~ VILLAGE INN ~

The Oaks, Henniker, NH 03242
TEL (603) 4283281; (800) 5310330 FAX (603) 429218
E-MAIL info@colbyhillinn.com WEBSITE www.colbyhillinn.com

HENNIKER IS LIVELIER than many attractive New England towns, thanks to the students of New England College, whose most famous graduate is film star Geena Davis. She sometimes stays at the Colby Hill Inn, a classic 18thC house on the outskirts of town. What started as a coach stop in 1795 became a farmhouse, then reopened as an inn in 1960. The entrance has wood panelling and, more often than not, a jar of cookies. Although antiques abound, the effect is not overwhelming; the sitting-room has the sort of sofas and tables that are 'comfortable'. The same balance is achieved in the bedrooms. Not all are feminine; number 7 is a favourite with men thanks to its dark green decoration. With Concord nearby, businessmen have discovered this inn, so data ports have been installed in all rooms. Cyndi and Mason Cobb took over the inn in 2000, and have been joined by chef Eric Therrien. His menus range from classic onion soups and pâtés to chicken stuffed with lobster, leeks and Boursin. The restaurant is open to non-residents. The large swimming-pool, one of the best our inspector saw, is totally secluded: a barn on one side, countryside views on the other.

~

NEARBY Pat's Peak ski area; golf, Mt Sunapee State Park.
LOCATION on edge of town; car parking
FOOD breakfast, dinner
PRICE rooms $$-$$$ with breakfast
ROOMS 16 double; all have bath or shower, phone
FACILITIES 2 dining rooms, 2 sitting rooms; garden, swimming pool
SMOKING no
CREDIT CARDS AE, MC, V
CHILDREN over 7
DISABLED not suitable
CLOSED never
PROPRIETORS the Cobb family

NEW HAMPSHIRE

HENNIKER

THE MEETING HOUSE

~ CONVERTED MEETING HOUSE ~

35 Flanders Road, Henniker, NH 03242
TEL (603) 4283228 FAX (603) 4286334
E-MAIL meetinghouse@conknet.com WEBSITE www.conknet.com/meetinghouse

1995 MARKED the 225th birthday of this Meeting House, built by the citizens of Henniker. Today's residents meet in the 200-year old barn next door, now a well-known restaurant. Overnight visitors, however, may stay in the six bedrooms of this small inn near the entrance to Pat's Peak Ski Area. Two families are in charge: June and Bill Davis plus their daughter, Cheryl, and her husband, chef Peter Bakke. The conversion is 'a bit of a squeeze,' so there is no breakfast room; instead, a continental breakfast is brought to bedrooms, anytime after 8 am.

Bedrooms are small and tidy without being cramped, while New York City art gallery prints give a contemporary feel. Number 1, in browns and brass, is bright; the suite has an attractive queen-sized bed. There are thick towels in the practical bathrooms. Guests also have the use of a hot tub and sauna. By contrast, the barn restaurant is spacious. Diners have shown their appreciation in an unusual way over the years, by sending samples of sand from all over the world. Vials and packets are labelled from as far afield as Antarctica and two miles under the ocean off Venezuela. A glassed-in addition overlooks the ski area.

~

NEARBY Pat's Peak ski area, gold, Mount Sunapee State Park.
LOCATION just outside village; car parking
FOOD breakfast, dinner
PRICE rooms $-$$ with breakfast
ROOMS 6 double; all have bath or shower, air-conditioning
FACILITIES dining room, sitting room, sauna; garden
SMOKING no
CREDIT CARDS AE, MC, V
CHILDREN not suitable
DISABLED not suitable
CLOSED restaurant only, Mon, Tues
PROPRIETORS Davis family, Bakke family

NEW HAMPSHIRE

HOLDERNESS

MANOR ON GOLDEN POND

~ LUXURY HOTEL ~

Route 3, Holderness, NH 03245
TEL (603) 9683348; (800) 5452141 FAX (603) 9682116
E-MAIL manorinn@lr.net WEBSITE www.manorongoldenpond.com

IN AN AREA WHERE SIMPLER and more economical lodging prevails, the grandeur of the Manor comes as a surprise. Comparisons with an English country house are often made, despite the classically New England exterior, complete with columned porch. Inside, however, the legacy of wealthy Englishman Isaac Van Horn (who built this as a private home in 1907) remains: oak and cherry panelling in the sitting room, with English furniture, and a grand dining room, with leaded windows plus a marble and wood fireplace. The bedrooms are equally imposing. Buckingham, once the master bedroom, has ivory and taffeta fabrics; Mayfair, with its king-sized bed, has views of Squam Lake and a private deck for sunbathing. Bathrooms, however, owe nothing to England: modern, with plenty of thick towels.

In 1999, Brian and Mary Ellen Shields took the helm, along with their children and Dusty the dog. The latter ensure that a family atmosphere pervades this large 25-room business. Their new chef, Jeff Woolley, is building a reputation for his New American cuisine in the grand restaurant. All in all, this hotel no longer needs to trade on the movie title annexed by a previous owner.

~

NEARBY Lakes Region, golf; winter sports.
LOCATION above Squam Lake; car parking
FOOD breakfast, dinner
PRICE rooms $$$-$$$$ with breakfast
ROOMS 25 double; all have bath or shower
FACILITIES dining room, sitting room, bar; garden, swimming pool, tennis
SMOKING no
CREDIT CARDS AE, MC, V
CHILDREN over 12
DISABLED not suitable
CLOSED never
PROPRIETORS the Shields family

NEW HAMPSHIRE

JACKSON VILLAGE

INN AT THORN HILL

~ COUNTRY INN ~

Thorn Hill Road, Jackson Village, NH 03846
TEL (603) 3834242; (800) 2898990 FAX (603) 3838062
E-MAIL thornhill@ncia.net WEBSITE www.innatthornhill.com

ON A RISE ABOVE the picture-perfect village of Jackson, the popularity of this inn is a tribute to Jim and Ibby Cooper. There always seems to be something going on, such as the hugely popular wine or beer dinners, yet there is still time and space for those who want to do no more than admire Mount Washington, which dominates the landscape.

The main inn, designed by Stanford White back in 1895, has a wide porch and bright white wicker furniture. Inside, the Victorian atmosphere is tempered by modern good sense, "not too lacy or cute," according to one guest. A baby grand piano stands in the sitting room, a fireplace is the focal point of the pub, and the only television at the inn is in the parlour. Guests who want to avoid the Victorian-style bedrooms upstairs, opt for the converted Carriage House with its country feel, or one of the small cottages. The enthusiasm for food is reflected by the chefs who grow their own herbs and the waitresses who produce organic vegetables. Sweet pepper-crusted shrimp and braised salmon with mussels and a saffron broth are among the enterprising dishes that result. Don't ignore the well-priced low season packages.

~

NEARBY winter sports; golf, fishing, White Mountains.
LOCATION outside village; car parking
FOOD breakfast, dinner
PRICE rooms $$-$$$ with breakfast
ROOMS 19 double; all have bath or shower, phone
FACILITIES dining room, sitting room, bar; garden
SMOKING no
CREDIT CARDS not accepted
CHILDREN over 8
DISABLED not suitable
CLOSED never
PROPRIETORS Jim and Ibby Cooper

New Hampshire

JACKSON VILLAGE

Nestlenook Farm on the River

~ LUXURY BED-AND-BREAKFAST ~

Dinsmore Road, Jackson Village, NH 03846
TEL (603) 3839443; (800) 6599443 FAX (603) 3834515
E-MAIL nestlenk@ncia.net WEBSITE www.nestlenook.com

A BRASS PLAQUE at the gate says it all: 'A new romance – Nov 1989'. This is the sort of inn that guests either love or hate. Outside, the Victorian gingerbread verges on the excessive, with fences, arches and bridges everywhere. 'It seems as if there's a gazebo for every guest.' There is more decoration inside: locally-made cut and leaded glass illuminates the entrance, a Victorian birdcage in the parlour is filled with exotic finches.

Jackson has an artists' community of long standing and bedrooms are dedicated to locals like William Paskell and Frank Shapleigh. The C C Murdoch Suite, for four, fills the top floor and has views in three directions. The Myke Morton reflects the origins of the 200-year old building with beams, a brick hearth and a side porch. Jacuzzis are a matter of course in the plush bathrooms. City folk are introduced to horseback riding, their children to feeding deer. In winter, skaters whizz along Emerald Lake and warm up in the gazebo. An Austrian sleigh, drawn by two plodding English shire horses, gives another reminder of 'yesteryear'. There have been changes since the Cyrs opened in 1989; they closed the restaurant and now welcome families with older children.

~

NEARBY winter sports; golf, fishing, White Mountains.
LOCATION off Rte 16; car parking
FOOD breakfast
PRICE rooms $$-$$$$ with breakfast
ROOMS 7 double; 2 suites; all have bath or shower, air-conditioning, phone
FACILITIES dining room, sitting room, bar; garden, heated swimming pool
SMOKING no
CREDIT CARDS AE, MC, V
CHILDREN over 12
DISABLED not suitable
CLOSED never
PROPRIETORS Robert and Nancy Cyr

NEW HAMPSHIRE

PETERBOROUGH

APPLE GATE
~ RURAL BED-AND-BREAKFAST ~

199 Upland Farm Road, Peterborough, NH 03458
TEL (603) 9246543; (800) 2580330 FAX (603) 2788838
E-MAIL d@applegatenh.mv.com WEBSITE www.nhlodging.org

PETERBOROUGH is a classic small town, so much so that Thornton Wilder wrote a play about it back in the 1930s, called Our Town. Today, there are bookstores, crafts and art shops. Not far from town, across the lane from an apple orchard, is the Apple Gate, a pretty, yet unpretentious place to stay. And that is its charm. Owners Ken and Dianne Legenhausen left Long Island with a plan: "So many bed-and-breakfasts have become fancy, very expensive places to stay. We just want to be clean, comfortable and reasonable." They have succeeded; this is a classic in the bed-and-breakfast genre.

Outside, a broad wrap-around porch is set with welcoming rocking chairs. Inside, the theme is apples, with stencils running up the walls, and rooms named for four popular varieties: Crispin, Cortland, Granny Smith and McIntosh. In the bedrooms and small sitting-room, furniture is old, rather than antique, "so that guests aren't afraid of touching anything, or to sit down and relax." Breakfast is a sociable affair, served at a large table where savvy guests always ask if Dianne is preparing her soufflé-like German pancakes, topped with apples.

~

NEARBY Mt Monadnock; Sharon Arts Center; hiking.
LOCATION in country; car parking
FOOD breakfast
PRICE rooms $-$$ with breakfast
ROOMS 4; all have bath or shower
FACILITIES dining room, sitting room
SMOKING no
CREDIT CARDS AE, MC, V
CHILDREN over 12
DISABLED not suitable
CLOSED never
PROPRIETORS Ken and Dianne Legenhausen

NEW HAMPSHIRE

TAMWORTH

TAMWORTH INN

~ VILLAGE INN ~

Main Street, Tamworth, NH 03886
TEL (603) 3237721; (800) 6427352 FAX (253) 550 3204

GROVER CLEVELAND, president of the United States more than a century ago, used to spend his summers in this village. Although it has all the ingredients of a New England postcard (general store, 1792 church with impressive spire, a river plus an inn) it is not on the main tourist trails. Most visitors come in summer to see the Barnstormers summer theatre founded by Cleveland's son.

The Tamworth Inn is the heart of the community. Dating from 1833, this unspoilt Victorian building is on three floors. The top bedrooms, high up under the roof, have mansard windows. Inside, all is freshly-polished tidiness. Since the Schraders arrived in 1998, they have carefully redecorated, adding two luxury suites. A handsome Federal mirror hangs on one wall, a collection of old sleds decorates the pub. In bedrooms number 1, an itinerant artist painted the murals back in the 1930s, as payment for his stay. He also painted some of the furniture. The yellow barn at the back was the birthplace of the Barnstormers; today it is the restaurant, open to the public, with an eclectic menu: crab cakes with chipotle aioli, soy ginger marinated chicken with apricot glaze, vegetable ravioli with a vodka tomato sauce.

~

NEARBY hiking, Mt Chocorua; cross-country and downhill skiing.
LOCATION in village; car parking
FOOD breakfast, dinner
PRICE rooms $$ with breakfast
ROOMS 16; all have bath or shower
FACILITIES dining room, sitting room, bar; garden, swimming pool
SMOKING no
CREDIT CARDS AE, MC, V
CHILDREN over 7
DISABLED not suitable
CLOSED never
PROPRIETORS Virginia and Bob Schrader

NEW HAMPSHIRE

WEST CHESTERFIELD

CHESTERFIELD INN

～ COUNTRY INN ～

Route 9, West Chesterfield, NH 03466
TEL (603) 2563211; (800) 3655515 FAX (603) 2566131
E-MAIL chstinn@sover.net WEBSITE www.chesterfieldinn.com

ALMOST ON THE VERMONT border, this inn is set back from busy Route 9 but 'has a grand view across the Connecticut River.' Phil and Judy Hueber took over in 1987 and have renovated with respect for the building's 200-year history. For guests who want to mingle, the sitting room is the social centre, with its natural wood-panelled walls, brass chandelier and high cathedral ceiling. In winter, the large, red, wood-fired stove in a two-storey brick wall adds a cheery touch.

Forget the dated bathrooms of many inns, these boast new fixtures and fittings, with Jacuzzi-style tubs and fluffy towels. Bedrooms are generous in size, with well-chosen plain and patterned fabrics. Some have a private balcony or open on to a patio, others a working fireplace.

Improvements in 1994 made the dining room more attractive. Chef Glen Gonyea's innovative, 'new' New England cuisine ranges from a pumpkin risotto to venison with a port and cranberry sauce or a succulent honey hazelnut pork tenderloin. All this does not come cheaply, but is worth it for a special weekend. 'Stylish' was the overall verdict.

～

NEARBY hiking; Mt Monadnock; Brattleboro; winter sports.
LOCATION off Rte 9; car parking
FOOD breakfast, dinner
PRICE rooms $$-$$$$ with breakfast
ROOMS 13 double; 2 suites; all have bath or shower, air-conditioning, phone, TV
FACILITIES dining room, sitting room
SMOKING no
CREDIT CARDS AE, MC, V
CHILDREN welcome
DISABLED not suitable
CLOSED never
PROPRIETORS Phil and Judy Hueber

MAINE

BAR HARBOR

BALANCE ROCK

~ OCEANSIDE INN ~

21 Albert Meadow, Bar Harbor, ME 04609
TEL (207) 2882610; (800) 7530494 FAX (207) 2885534
E-MAIL barhbrinns@aol.com WEBSITE www.barharborvacations.com

A CENTURY AGO, a Scottish tycoon commissioned top architects to build a 'cottage', or summer home, for his family. It was one of many in this fashionable resort, but the view was one of the best. It still is impressive: overlooking Frenchman Bay, with pampered lawns running down to the famous Shore Path. Yet, Balance Rock is only one block away from the middle of town. So, guests here have the best of both worlds: the shops and restaurants as well as peace and privacy.

Today's owners have recreated the glories of the past, which are pointed out by the concierge who shows arriving guests round. He points out the modern touches, such as a heated outdoor swimming pool and the Veranda Bar where you can light up a cigar. The most expensive rooms have ocean views and a Jacuzzi, fireplace or deck; or a combination of these luxuries. Or, perhaps, a sauna! Even the least expensive room, however, has its own small but private porch. The breakfast buffet is from 8 to 10 am and guests usually take their trays out on to the veranda. More mini-hotel than cosy bed-and-breakfast, this inn is a special occasion place, with prices to match.

~

NEARBY Acadia National Park; outdoor activities.
LOCATION on ocean; car parking
FOOD breakfast
PRICE rooms $-$$$$ with breakfast
ROOMS 16; all have bath or shower
FACILITIES dining room, sitting room; swimming pool
SMOKING restricted
CREDIT CARDS AE, MC, V
CHILDREN welcome
DISABLED not suitable
CLOSED Nov to April
MANAGER Molly Grant

MAINE

BAR HARBOR

INN AT BAY LEDGE

~ CLIFFTOP INN ~

1385 Sand Point Road, Bar Harbor, ME 04609
TEL (207) 2884204 FAX (207) 2885573
E-MAIL bayledge@downeast.net WEBSITE www.innatbayledge.com

BAR HARBOR, a summer playground for the rich a century ago, still draws vacationers from around the world. It stands at the entrance to Acadia National Park, one of America's most popular and beautiful scenic attractions. The park is on Mount Desert Island and the combination of ocean and mountains is stunning. With 120 miles of trails, it is easy to explore on foot or mountain bike. About five miles from town, the inn stands among pine trees on top of an 80-foot cliff; the lodge-style building has terraces, gardens and a long porch, with inviting wicker chairs. The cheerful interior has pine panelling, fireplaces and picture windows. All but one bedroom have exceptional water views. Once the home of a minister, there is enough history for each bedroom to merit a name, explained in books by the bed. Three rustic cottages, even deeper in the forest, provide extra seclusion. Eighty wooden steps lead down to a private beach, where guests explore The Ovens, the caves once used by Native Americans. Go whale watching, sea kayaking with Maine guides, and, of course, explore the park.

~

NEARBY Acadia National Park; outdoor activities.
LOCATION in forest; car parking
FOOD breakfast, dinner
PRICE rooms $$ with breakfast
ROOMS 10; all have bath or shower
FACILITIES dining room, sitting room; swimming pool
SMOKING no
CREDIT CARDS MC, V
CHILDREN welcome
DISABLED not suitable
CLOSED Nov to April
PROPRIETORS Jack and Jeani Ochtera

MAINE

BAR HARBOUR

MANOR HOUSE

~ VICTORIAN BED-AND-BREAKFAST ~

106 West Street, Bar Harbor, ME 04609
TEL (207) 2883759; (800) 4370088 FAX (207) 2882974
E-MAIL manor@acadia.net WEBSITE www.barharbormanorhouse.com

THERE IS A VICTORIAN atmosphere in this many-gabled, 1887 mansion that is on the National Register of Historic Places. Mac Noyes is a local and many of the antiques here are from his own family. There are oriental carpets on polished floors, plus bureaux and clocks, but beds are a particular feature: many have high, elaborate head and foot boards. Most rooms have wallpaper, varying from a delicate floral band to all-over patterns of deep blue or burgundy. On our arrival, there were Greek, German, English as well as American guests, many sitting on the large porch and chatting over afternoon refreshments.

Set back from the main street, the lawns and house are protected by tall hedges. With two sitting rooms plus a television room, this would suit those wanting privacy as well as those wanting conviviality. Bedrooms vary in size, from the generous to the cramped; some have working fireplaces. Most bathrooms are en suite; bathrobes are provided in the three whose baths are across the hall. In the Chauffeur's Cottage, one entire floor is the Honeymoon suite; the two cottages are modern, with kitchenettes. Blueberries in the muffins at breakfast are from the Noyes' family farm.

~

NEARBY Acadia National Park; whale-watching, canoeing, hiking.
LOCATION in town; car parking
FOOD breakfast
PRICE rooms $-$$ with breakfast
ROOMS 18; all have bath or shower; TV in cottages
FACILITIES 3 sitting rooms; porch, garden
SMOKING no
CREDIT CARDS AE, MC, V
CHILDREN over 8
DISABLED not suitable
CLOSED Nov to May
PROPRIETOR Mac Noyes

MAINE

BAR HARBOR

MAPLES INN

～ BED-AND-BREAKFAST ～

16 Roberts Avenue, Bar Harbor, ME 04609
TEL (207) 2883443 FAX (207) 2880356
E-MAIL info@maplesinn.com WEBSITE www.acadia.net/maples

TOM AND SUE PALUMBO claim an eccentric record: they are the third in a succession of guests to have bought this inn. "We stayed here eight times before buying it in 1998." They have added air-conditioning, redecorated and now all the rooms have their own bathrooms. They have also extended their season, as guests discover the delights of winter in Acadia National Park, just a few minutes away by car. "There are miles and miles of carriageways, ideal for cross-country skiing and snow-shoeing." Sue's gourmet breakfast provides fuel for this exercise, with blueberry stuffed French toast in much demand. Less energetic souls read in front of the fire or on the porch.

The street is named for the doctor who built this summer home back in 1903; bedrooms, however, are named for trees. Red Oak is the most popular, since the deck outside is actually a tree house. English Holly has a small step-stool for climbing into the high four-poster bed, while White Birch is a two-room suite. Of course, the national park is popular in summer and fall as well, with visitors enjoying the peace as well as the wide variety of sporting activities.

～

NEARBY water sports; winter sports, Acadia National Park.
LOCATION in town; car parking
FOOD breakfast
PRICE rooms $-$$ with breakfast
ROOMS 5 double; 1 suite; all have bath or shower, radio
FACILITIES dining room, sitting room
SMOKING no
CREDIT CARDS MC, V
CHILDREN over 12
DISABLED not suitable
CLOSED never
PROPRIETORS Sue and Tom Palumbo

MAINE

BAR HARBOR

MIRA MONTE

BED-AND-BREAKFAST MANSION

69 Mount Desert Street, Bar Harbor, ME 04609
TEL (207) 2884263; (800) 5535109 FAX (207) 2883115
E-MAIL mburns@miramonte.com WEBSITE www.miramonte.com

WINGS, BALCONIES, side entrances and brick terraces have been added on since a wealthy Philadelphian family built this 'summer cottage' in 1864. In 1980, the house was going to become a funeral parlour; it was rescued and turned into a bed-and-breakfast by Marian Burns, that rarity among innkeepers: a real local. Her rummages around barn sales and estate auctions for old furniture and pictures for the inn have resulted in a 'comfort without frills' look that suits this vacation spot. The library is the real thing with plenty of books and deep, stuffed chairs and on cool summer evenings a log fire is lit.

Breakfast can be a social meal at the long dining room table, or you can take your tray up to your balcony, out to the porch or into the side-garden with its statues and walkways. The name, 'Behold the mountains', refers to Cadillac Mountain and the Acadia National Park hills, which are 'right out front.' Marian knows the trails and can recommend the best places to hike. She also hates smoking and threatens a $35 fine for anyone who lights up in their bedroom. The three suites in a separate building have less character; we advise staying in the main house.

NEARBY whale watching, canoeing, hiking.
LOCATION in town; car parking
FOOD breakfast
PRICE rooms $-$$$ with breakfast
ROOMS 12 double; 3 suites; all have bath or shower, air-conditioning, phone, TV, radio
FACILITIES dining room, sitting room; garden
SMOKING no
CREDIT CARDS AE, MC, V
CHILDREN not suitable
DISABLED 1 room
CLOSED Nov to April
PROPRIETOR Marian Burns

MAINE

BAR HARBOR

PRIMROSE INN

〜 VICTORIAN BED-AND-BREAKFAST 〜

73 Mt Desert Street, Bar Harbor, ME 04609
TEL (207) 2884031; (877) 8463424 FAX (207) 2889749
E-MAIL relax@primroseinn.com WEBSITE www.primroseinn.com

READERS ARE HAPPY to report that this inn has had a new lease of life since 1998. That's when the enthusiastic computer-experts-turned-innkeepers, Bryan Stevens and Pamela Parker, took over. They repainted rooms, laid new carpets and installed air-conditioning. The result is that bedrooms are now light, bright and flowery, a far cry from the days when this was originally a guest-house for the first Episcopal Bishop of Maine. Another former owner was Timothee Adamowski, conductor of the Boston Pops Orchestra, who used to hold musical evenings in the formal parlour.

Readers also report that food is a major passion in the house. Pamela admits that she hides in the kitchen, baking, "while Bryan smiles in the dining room." Breakfasts are lavish, including side dishes as well as desserts: ginger pear pancakes with maple syrup, sausages and blackberry-glazed fruit compote. Even the ham and smoked salmon are smoked at the inn. In the afternoon, tea is laid out with four or five baked goods, from raspberry fudge brownies to Amaretto cheesecake. Expect iced tea in summer; hot mulled cider when it gets chilly.

〜

NEARBY water-sports; Acadia National Park.
LOCATION on main street; car parking
FOOD breakfast
PRICE rooms $-$$ with breakfast
ROOMS 9 double; 5 suites; all have bath or shower, phone, TV
FACILITIES dining room, sitting room
SMOKING no
CREDIT CARDS AE, MC, V
CHILDREN very welcome
DISABLED not suitable
CLOSED Nov to April
PROPRIETORS Bryan Stevens and Pamela Parker

MAINE

BAR HARBOR

ULLIKANA

~ BED-AND-BREAKFAST INN ~

16 The Field, Bar Harbor, ME 04609
TEL (207) 2889552 FAX (207) 2883682
WEBSITE www.ullikana.com

CARE MUST BE TAKEN TO find this since The Field is an unmarked street that looks like the entrance to the Bar Harbor Banking and Trust. At the end, however, stands this Tudor-style house that could be an illustration in an English story book for children. Roy Kasindorf and French-Canadian Hélène Harton were living in New York City when they visited Maine and "immediately connected with the spirit of Ullikana." Both are art-lovers and most of the paintings and sculptures are by friends. Books on artists are stacked on the large coffee table in the sitting room, where serious poker games were held by a previous owner. Another was Boston sea-merchant, Alpheus Hardy. Having built Bar Harbor's first summer home, he created this in 1885.

Of the bedrooms, number six has a private porch with views through trees to boats sailing in and out of the harbor; number five, the Red Room is cheerful with gingham curtains and red-patterned wallpaper. Bathrooms are small, except for the two that are not *en suite*; these look Victorian, with claw-foot tubs and dark walls brightened by big windows. Overall, the feeling is secluded, yet this is just a short walk from the middle of the village.

~

NEARBY Frenchman's Bay, Acadia National Park.
LOCATION near Main Street; car parking
FOOD breakfast
PRICE rooms $$-$$$ with breakfast
ROOMS 8 double; 2 family; all have bath or shower
FACILITIES dining room, sitting room; garden
SMOKING no
CREDIT CARDS MC, V
CHILDREN over 8
DISABLED not suitable
CLOSED Nov to May
PROPRIETORS Hélène Harton and Roy Kasindorf

MAINE

BLUE HILL

BLUE HILL INN
~ RESTAURANT-INN ~

Union Street, Blue Hill, ME 04614
TEL (207) 3742844; (800) 8267415 FAX (207) 3742829
E-MAIL mary@bluehillinn.com WEBSITE www.bluehillinn.com

THIS WAS BUILT by a blacksmith in 1830, then traded to his brother-in-law, a sea-captain. It has been an inn since 1840, possibly the oldest in continuous operation in Maine, and had the first indoor W.C. in Blue Hill, installed in 1927. Mary and Don Hartley were living in Ohio when they decided to become innkeepers; after years searching three New England states, they discovered this inn, bought it immediately and the guests woke up to new owners. That was in 1987. Out went the plastic flowers, in came carefully-chosen antiques which create an atmosphere that is elegant but not too formal.

The Hartleys are the sort of innkeepers who make the job look easy. Each evening they host a reception where drinks and hors d'oeuvres are served and guests can chat. There are restaurants within walking distance, but four times a year, the Hartleys organize popular wine dinners, featuring best of local and Maine-grown organic produce and seafood. Flowers and herbs come straight from the garden. The breakfast menu ranges from blueberry pancakes to omelettes. Blue Hill is home to craftsmen and musicians, and the Kneisel Hall school of music holds summer concerts.

~

NEARBY Acadia National Park; whale watching, ferry trips.
LOCATION in village; car parking
FOOD breakfast
PRICE rooms $$-$$$ with breakfast
ROOMS 12; all have bath or shower
FACILITIES dining room, 2 sitting rooms; garden
SMOKING no
CREDIT CARDS MC, V
CHILDREN not suitable
DISABLED 1 room
CLOSED Nov to April
PROPRIETORS Mary and Don Hartley

MAINE

CAMDEN

BELMONT

~ RESTAURANT-INN ~

6 Belmont Avenue, Camden, ME 04843
TEL (207) 2368053; (800) 2388053
E-MAIL info@thebelmontinn.com WEBSITE www.thebelmontinn.com

CAMDEN IS a popular town, with a harbour full of boats and a main street lined with historic houses, many of which are bed-and-breakfasts. Off on a side street stands this grey century-old building with rounded tables and a porch. Unusually among inns of this size, it has a restaurant, open to the public as well as to guests. Chefs Scott Marquis and Rebecca Brown took over the restaurant in 1999, and the inn itself in 2001.

Few changes were needed in the inn. All the bedrooms are simple, yet tasteful in an elegant way; they are also free of the usual pot-pourris and knick-knacks, so "staying here is not like visiting your grandmother." By contrast, the restaurant is quite grand, with linens and crystal. The 'innovative American' dishes, too, are complex. Musts include crab cakes with a chipotle scallion mayonnaise and steamed lobster wonton with lemon grass, though locals sated with seafood clamour for rack of lamb. Scott also smokes everything from salmon and duck legs to tomatoes and almonds. Rebecca bakes breads and creates desserts, such as a chocolate ganache with whole macadamia nuts and warm caramel. More reports, please, on this small gem.

NEARBY Mount Battie, state park; water-sports; seal watching.
LOCATION in town; car parking
FOOD breakfast, dinner
PRICE rooms $$ with breakfast
ROOMS 5 double; 1 suite; all have bath or shower
FACILITIES dining room, sitting room, bar; garden
SMOKING no
CREDIT CARDS MC, V
CHILDREN over 10
DISABLED not suitable
CLOSED weekdays in winter
PROPRIETORS Scott Marquis and Rebecca Brown

MAINE

CAMDEN

CAMDEN MAINE STAY

~ HISTORIC BED-AND-BREAKFAST ~

22 High Street, Camden, ME 04843
TEL (207) 2369636 FAX (207) 2360621
E-MAIL innkeeper@camdenmainestay.com WEBSITE www.camdenmainestay.com

"I COULD HAVE STAYED and chatted all day; I felt instantly at home here." That is high praise indeed from our inspector, who has seen hundreds of bed-and-breakfasts all over New England. So what makes this one so special? The house dates from 1802, and comes with pumpkin pine floors, interesting antiques, Oriental rugs and fireplaces. With three sitting rooms, there is more public space than in many inns. Each bedroom is different, furnished with pretty printed wallpapers. Some have themes, such as the Rackham Room, with its original works by the illustrator of Wind in the Willows. At the top of the house, the Stitchery Suite is useful for a family; most romantic has to be the Carriage House Room, with an iron stove and separate entrance. Don't expect swathes of fabric draping beds or dramatic decoration; the overall look here is traditional and pleasingly homey. Guests pop into the large kitchen and grab a cookie or collect some ice; they take coffee out into the 2-acre garden. But the main secret of the success of this inn is the innkeepers: Peter Smith and his wife, Donny, plus her twin sister Diana Robson. Experienced innkeepers, their genuine welcome turns first-timers into regulars.

~

NEARBY Mt Battie, harbour, water-sports.
LOCATION on main street; own car parking
FOOD breakfast
PRICE rooms $-$$ with breakfast
ROOMS 8 double; all have bath or shower, radio, hairdrier; some TV, fireplaces
FACILITIES dining room, 3 sitting rooms; sun porch, garden
SMOKING no
CREDIT CARDS AE, MC, V
CHILDREN over 12
DISABLED not suitable
CLOSED never
PROPRIETORS Peter and Donny Smith, Diana Robson

MAINE

CAMDEN

NORUMBEGA

∾ LUXURY BED-AND-BREAKFAST ∾

61 High Street, Camden, ME 04843
TEL (207) 2364646 FAX (207) 2364990
E-MAIL stay@norumbegainn.com WEBSITE www.norumbegainn.com

NOT ALL THE STATELY summer homes of Maine are in Bar Harbor. Joseph Stearns made a fortune selling his telegraphy system to Western Union, then toured Europe and came home to design this strange amalgamation of Scottish, English and French architectural styles. That was in 1886; now his virgin view of Penobscot Bay is punctuated by a few buildings down the hill and more traffic passes by on the main coastal road, Route 1.

More baronial than royal, this 'castle' impresses with hand-carved oak, decorative inlay, a grand piano in the Music Room and a massive table in the dining-room. Bedrooms, with names such as Windsor, Versailles and Balmoral, are furnished in the 'no expense-spared' designer-style one would expect for these prices. The Library Suite, in forest green with a red tartan sofa, has a mahogany gallery providing an upper level, while the Penthouse, the entire width of the house, has a private deck and panoramic vista. Dinner is restricted to house guests and features grand dishes, such as sea bass with garlic and Dijon cream sauce or steak with a hazelnut sauce. When you want something different for a special occasion, this could be it.

∾

NEARBY water-sports, fishing, cycling; state park.
LOCATION just out of Camden; car parking
FOOD breakfast, dinner
PRICE rooms $$-$$$$ with breakfast
ROOMS 13; all have bath or shower, phone, hairdrier
FACILITIES dining room, 3 sitting rooms, billiard room; garden
SMOKING no
CREDIT CARDS AE, MC, V
CHILDREN over 7
DISABLED not suitable
CLOSED never
MANAGER Joanne Reuillard

MAINE

CAMDEN

WINDWARD HOUSE

~ HISTORIC BED-AND-BREAKFAST ~

6 High Street, Camden, ME 04843
TEL (207) 2369656 FAX (207) 2300433
E-MAIL bnb@windwardhouse.com WEBSITE www.windwardhouse.com

JON AND MARY DAVIES are a tough act to follow. The couple that made the Windward House famous may have retired but the Lawrences have a pretty good track record, too. They ran an inn in Vermont for many years before switching to the coast for a change. Since 1999, they have completely upgraded the bedrooms in the 1854 house, adding gas log fires, Jacuzzi tubs and decks. Carefully concealed are air-conditioning, cable TV, data ports and, most of all, soundproofing. Guests also approve of the special allergy-free featherbeds. Already there are regular requests for the Mount Battie room, with views of the famous mountain, and the Silver Birch suite, new in 2001. This one has a large living room, separate bedroom, deck and easy ground floor access.

Del Lawrence is the breakfast chef, with a vast repertoire. "Guests can eat anytime they want between 8 and 9.30 and order from seven or eight choices off the menu." Popular dishes range from fancy Belgian waffles and orange yoghurt pancakes to the simple pleasures few people bother to cook at home: good old poached eggs, sausage and bacon.

~

NEARBY Mount Battie, state park, water-sports; seal watching.
LOCATION in town; car parking
FOOD breakfast
PRICE rooms 8; all have bath or shower
ROOMS 8; all have bath or shower
FACILITIES dining room, 3 sitting rooms; garden
SMOKING no
CREDIT CARDS AE, MC, V
CHILDREN over 12
DISABLED not suitable
CLOSED never
PROPRIETORS Del and Charlotte Lawrence

MAINE

CASTINE

CASTINE INN
∾ RESTAURANT-INN ∾

Main Street, Castine, ME 04421
TEL (207) 3264365 FAX (207) 3264570
E-MAIL relax@castineinn.com WEBSITE www.castineinn.com

THIS IS A FINE EXAMPLE of a Maine summer hotel, built in 1898 for 'rusticators', the summer visitors from Boston, New York City and Philadelphia, who would stay for weeks or even months. Guests sit on the wrap-around porch and watch the comings and goings on elm-lined Main Street. They also enjoy the formal gardens full of iris, roses and clematis, which thrive "because the climate is similar to England's," according to staff. There is a grape arbour, a little bridge, even a knot garden.

A previous owner was also an artist. In the dining room, she recreated the town of Castine in a mural covering several walls. It makes a fitting backdrop for Tom Gutow's imaginative cuisine, featuring local ingredients. Expect grilled *foie gras* with candied rhubarb, olive crusted salmon with caponata, sweetbreads with a potato leek cake and desserts such as raspberry crème brûlée. The platter of French cheeses is a reminder of Tom's stints with great chefs in French kitchens. Upstairs, the bedrooms on the top floor are larger and more expensive than others; some have water views. Many bathrooms have old-fashioned claw-foot tubs.

∾

NEARBY harbour, fishing; Fort George; summer theatre.
LOCATION near harbour; car parking
FOOD breakfast, dinner
PRICE rooms $$ with breakfast
ROOMS 15 double; 3 suites; 2 family; all have bath or shower
FACILITIES 2 dining rooms, sitting room, bar, sauna; garden
SMOKING no
CREDIT CARDS MC, V
CHILDREN over 5
DISABLED not suitable
CLOSED Nov to April
PROPRIETORS Tom and Amy Gutow

MAINE

CASTINE

THE PENTAGÖET INN

~ SUMMER MANSION ~

Main Street, Castine, ME 04421
TEL (207) 3268616; (800) 8451701 FAX (207) 3269382
E-MAIL pentagoet@pentagoet.com WEBSITE www.pentagoet.com

CASTINE IS NOW A PRETTY, sleepy village but it was the home of the English fleet during the war with the French in Canada in the 1760s; the Maine Maritime Academy continues the nautical tradition. The inn, built in 1894, was bought by Jack Burke and Julie VandeGraaf in 2000; they totally transformed it, putting the accent on informality and relaxation. Jack was in the Foreign Service and his collection of political memorabilia from his travels is a feature. The focus is Passports Pub, like an old colonial club, with floor to ceiling photographs of 20thC world leaders peering down at the rattan chairs. Classical jazz, another hobby, plays along in the background.

Julie ran a patisserie in Philadelphia, so her territory is the deep pink dining room. Breakfasts come with fresh fruit, eggs and home made sausage, as well as Julie's pastries. Dinner is served by candlelight, with flowers from the abundant garden. Fresh local seafood is used in the bouillabaisse, Maine crab cakes, and lobster and scallop pie. Extra touches include jugs of coffee outside your door at 7am and Bermuda bicycles, complete with baskets, so you can pedal out to the lighthouse with a picnic.

~

NEARBY fishing; Fort George; summer theatre; national parks.
LOCATION in village; public car parking
FOOD breakfast, dinner
PRICE rooms $$-$$$ with breakfast
ROOMS 16; all have bath or shower
FACILITIES dining room, sitting room, library; garden
SMOKING no
CREDIT CARDS MC, V
CHILDREN over 16
DISABLED not suitable
CLOSED Nov to April
PROPRIETORS Jack Burke and Julie VandeGraaf

MAINE

DEER ISLE

GOOSE COVE LODGE

~ WATERSIDE INN ~

Deer Isle, Sunset, ME 04683
TEL (207) 3482508 FAX (207) 3482624
E-MAIL goosecove@goosecovelodge.com WEBSITE www.goosecovelodge.com

THIS IS TOTALLY DIFFERENT to other inns in this guide. The location is more away from it all than most, on a rocky cove bordered by pines but with sandy beaches for swimming. The grounds are extensive, with numerous hiking trails at low tide, access to an island nature reserve. There are daily walks, led by owner Dom Parisi, another naturalist or perhaps a local geologist. This tradition dates back to 1947 when the lodge was opened by a botanist. There is also canoeing and kayaking.

Accommodation here is simple and rustic: secluded cottages dotted around the property, plus suites and bedrooms in two annexes and also some attached cottages. The main lodge is log cabin-style, with pine panelling and a huge stone fireplace. The telescope is powerful enough to show the moons of Jupiter.

From 5.30 pm to 8 pm, children under 12 eat separately, supervised and entertained by baby-sitters. Meanwhile, adults have time to themselves, gathering for drinks and dinner followed by, perhaps, a concert of classical or folk music, or a talk by a local artist or lobster fisherman. In summer, bookings for cabins are by the week, on a bed-and-breakfast basis.

~

NEARBY Isle au Haut ferry; Haystack Mountain School of Crafts.
LOCATION 5 km from village; car parking
FOOD breakfast, dinner
PRICE rooms $$ with breakfast
ROOMS 23; all have bath or shower; some fireplaces
FACILITIES dining room, 2 sitting rooms, library, bar; beach
SMOKING no
CREDIT CARDS AE, MC, V
CHILDREN welcome
DISABLED access possible
CLOSED Nov to April
PROPRIETORS Dom and Joanne Parisi

MAINE

DEER ISLE

PILGRIM'S INN

~ HISTORIC INN ~

Deer Isle, ME 04627
TEL (207) 3486615; (888) 7787505 FAX (207) 3487769
E-MAIL innkeeper@pilgrimsinn.com WEBSITE www.pilgrimsinn.com

"JUST ENOUGH but not too much rusticity." "More than plain and simple but not fancy." Those are the reactions of two guests who stayed in this inn, built in 1793 by Squire Ignatius Haskell for his wife, who came from Newburyport, Massachusetts and had ideas of grandeur in the back woods of Maine. Current innkeepers are Dan and Michele Brown, who took over in 2001, have upgraded all rooms to have private bathrooms, otherwise few changes were needed.

The chef, aims to use local ingredients and there is a set main course each night. This could be salmon, lobster and crab, or lamb; in summer, the outdoor grill may be used. Guests choose to eat at individual tables or join up with new friends; non-residents may also dine here. The dining room was originally the barn but was moved and joined on to the main house, though the farm-feel remains with implements on the walls, plain board walls, beams and a wood-burning stove. Bedrooms have a country look; bathrooms tend to be small, even cupboard-size, but towels are high-quality. There are antiques throughout, with "an almost English ambience."

~

NEARBY Haystack Mountain School of Crafts; hiking; boating.
LOCATION in village; car parking
FOOD breakfast, dinner
PRICE rooms $$-$$$
ROOMS 13, 2 cottages
FACILITIES dining room, 4 sitting rooms, bar; garden
SMOKING no
CREDIT CARDS MC, V
CHILDREN over 12
DISABLED not suitable
CLOSED never
PROPRIETORS Dan and Michele Brown

MAINE

EAST BOOTHBAY

FIVE GABLES INN

~ SEASIDE BED-AND-BREAKFAST ~

Murray Hill Road, East Boothbay, ME 04544
TEL (207) 6334551; (800) 4515048
E-MAIL info@fivegablesinn.com WEBSITE www.fivegablesinn.com

THERE ARE THREE 'Boothbays'. Most famous is Boothbay Harbor, crowded in summer, with shops and restaurants. East Boothbay is smaller and old-fashioned. Built in 1845 as a guest house, this inn looks out to Perch Island, a rocky outcrop in Linekin Bay.

De and Mike, the gregarious owners, enjoy nothing more than advising guests on what to do: go out on a windjammer or whale watching, picnic on an island or play golf. Strenuous exercise is essential after breakfast. Mike's buffets would be impressive with just the home-made granola, fruit and Southern-style biscuits. But, as a graduate of the Culinary Institute of America, he also serves up crème brûlée French toast with a raspberry sauce, mushroom quiche and baked apples in puff pastry.

Two of the three staircases are at the back, so guests can come and go without disturbing others in the sitting room, with its fireplace and picture windows. All but one of the bedrooms have water views; some have working fireplaces; each is decorated differently, with toning colours and patterns. Number 14, the largest, looks over the water, as does the snug number 16, high under a gable. Ideal for couples.

~

NEARBY boating, cycling, swimming; ferry to Monhegan Island.
LOCATION on the bay; car parking
FOOD breakfast
PRICE rooms $$ with breakfast
ROOMS 15 double; all have bath or shower, radio
FACILITIES dining room/sitting room, porch; garden
SMOKING no
CREDIT CARDS MC, V
CHILDREN over 12
DISABLED not suitable
CLOSED Nov to mid-May
PROPRIETORS De and Mike Kennedy

MAINE

HANCOCK POINT

CROCKER HOUSE

~ COUNTRY INN ~

Hancock Point, ME 04640
TEL (207) 4226806 FAX (207) 4223105
E-MAIL crocker@acadia.net WEBSITE www.acadia.net/crocker

DOWN A SEEMINGLY ENDLESS finger of land that is typical of the Maine coastline is Hancock Point. Only a small community now, in its heyday a century ago this was the terminus of the Bar Harbor railway with some 10,000 visitors arriving daily, then taking the ferry across to fashionable Bar Harbor. Passenger services stopped in the 1930s and now this inn, built in 1884, is the only remnant of those glory days.

When Richard Malaby bought the place in 1980, he owned a restaurant in Washington DC and had never lived in the country or near water. Here, all roads lead to the water and there is plenty of wildlife. Deer graze on the extensive lawn in front of the inn; a fox heads for the woods behind. Furnishings are country-comfortable, with wicker chairs and cheerful cushions in the sitting-room. Bedrooms tend to be small, with patterned wallpaper or decorative stencilling while some bathrooms are tiny. The large restaurant is open to non-residents; menus could include sea scallops, lamb or duck with a ginger Grand Marnier sauce. Sunday brunch served in summers. Potters, weavers and other craftsmen live in the area; Acadia National Park is a 35-minute drive away.

~

NEARBY tennis, cycling, sailing, fishing.
LOCATION in residential area; car parking
FOOD breakfast, dinner
PRICE rooms $-$$ with breakfast
ROOMS 11; all have bath or shower
FACILITIES 2 dining rooms, 2 sitting rooms, bar, hot tub; garden
SMOKING no
CREDIT CARDS AE, MC, V
CHILDREN welcome
DISABLED not suitable
CLOSED weekdays in winter
PROPRIETORS Richard and Elizabeth Malaby

MAINE

HANCOCK

LE DOMAINE

~ RESTAURANT-INN ~

Box 496, Hancock, ME 04640
TEL (207) 4223395; (800) 5548498 FAX (207) 4222316
E-MAIL nicole@ledomaine.com WEBSITE www.ledomaine.com

FEW RESTAURANTS IN THE USA can claim to be authentically French, but the Domaine's owner and chef, Nicole Purslow, learned from her legendary mother, Marianne Rose Dumas Purslow and still spends part of each winter in France. Classic dishes such as chicken roasted with garlic, salmon with lentils or liver Dijon-style are skilfully prepared and beautifully presented in a dining-room that looks almost Japanese, with its spare design, black highlights and polished wood floor. This same elegant, uncluttered style continues throughout the inn; staying here is a different experience from the heavily-decorated 'Victorian' inns.

The unprepossessing red house is separated from Route 1 by a high hedge; bedrooms are all at the back and are named after towns in Provence, so bright cushions and throws contrast with snowy white bedspreads and pale walls. The two suites have recently been redecorated. Towels are thick and brightly-coloured, floors are bare and polished. Regular guests enjoy breakfast on private decks, walks in the wood, rowing on the pond … and waiting for dinner. They feel the high standards justify the high prices.

~

NEARBY Mount Desert, Acadia National Park.
LOCATION on Rte 1; car parking
FOOD breakfast, dinner
PRICE rooms $$$-$$$$ with breakfast
ROOMS 5; all have bath or shower, radio
FACILITIES 3 dining rooms, sitting room, bar; garden
SMOKING restricted
CREDIT CARDS AE, MC, V
CHILDREN not suitable
DISABLED not suitable
CLOSED Nov to late May; restaurant only, Sun, Mon
PROPRIETOR Nicole Purslow

MAINE

KENNEBUNKPORT

CAPTAIN LORD MANSION

~ HISTORIC BED-AND-BREAKFAST ~

PO Box 800, Kennebunkport, ME 04046
TEL (207) 9673141; (800) 5223141 FAX (207) 9673172
E-MAIL innkeeper@captainlord.com WEBSITE www.captainlord.com

L IKE ANY 'CHARMING' seaside village, Kennebunkport is packed with
people in summer. The Bush family's vacation home is here and when
the President of the United States is here, the August crowds are swelled
by members of the press and White House staff. Things were different in
1814 when Nathaniel Lord, a merchant and ship-builder, built this
mansion on its prominent site. Bright yellow and topped by a cupola, it is
impossible to miss. The imposing, four-storey spiral staircase remains, as
do many hand-blown window pains. A huge 19thC coal stove dominates
the kitchen, where breakfast is served, family-style, in two sittings.
Sometimes the overflow is accommodated at the dining-table in the
largest sitting-room with its working music box.

Don't expect a hidden retreat: it is a well-known, busy inn with a
conference room and a gift shop plus 16 bedrooms in the main house. Bev
Davis and Rick Litchfield have built up this successful business since 1978,
restoring the house with quality antiques and traditional patterns. They also
own an 1807 federal house nearby, complete with four guest rooms for family
reunions or friends. Beach passes, towels and umbrellas are provided.

~

NEARBY water-sports, fishing, whale watching, cycling, tennis.
LOCATION in town; ample car parking
FOOD breakfast
PRICE rooms $$-$$$$ with breakfast
ROOMS 15 double; 1 suite; all have bath or shower, radio
FACILITIES 2 sitting rooms, television room; garden
SMOKING no
CREDIT CARDS MC, V
CHILDREN over 12
DISABLED not suitable
CLOSED never
PROPRIETORS Bev Davis and Rick Litchfield

MAINE

OLD FORT INN

~ COASTAL BED-AND-BREAKFAST ~

Old Fort Avenue, Kennebunkport, ME 04046
TEL (207) 9675353; (800) 8283678 FAX (207) 9674547
E-MAIL info@oldfortinn.com WEBSITE www.oldfortinn.com

IN ITS HEYDAY, Kennebunkport had some 30 imposing hotels where guest spent the summer but the Second World War put an end to that era. The main building here was originally the barn behind one of those hotels, which was torn down in the early 1960s. Bedrooms are in the large carriage house at the end of the garden. With a swimming-pool and tennis court, this inn has more facilities than many, so guests often stay for a week rather than just one night of a weekend.

It may seem odd to enter and find yourself in an antique shop but "many guests like to buy the silver, crystal or old linens," according to Sheila Aldrich. She had run a similar shop in San Francisco, so decided to continue the business when she and her husband, David, took over in 1980. The cash desk doubles as the reception for the inn, whose focal point is the high-ceilinged, 15-metre long sitting-room with a large brick fireplace, an old upright piano and plenty of sofas and chairs. In the carriage house, the hotel-like corridor is a 'fashion gallery', with framed antique clothes. Bedrooms vary in size and colour schemes but are all of a high standard, with modern bathrooms.

~

NEARBY water-sports, fishing, whale watching, cycling, tennis.
LOCATION off Ocean Avenue; car parking
FOOD breakfast
PRICE rooms $$-$$$$ with breakfast
ROOMS 14 double; 2 suites; all have bath or shower, phone, TV
FACILITIES sitting room; garden, swimming pool
SMOKING no
CREDIT CARDS AE, MC, V
CHILDREN over 12
DISABLED not suitable
CLOSED mid-Dec to mid-April
PROPRIETORS David and Sheila Aldrich

MAINE

KENNEBUNKPORT

WHITE BARN INN

~ LUXURY INN ~

Beach Street, Kennebunkport, ME 04046
TEL (207) 9672321 FAX (207) 9671100
E-MAIL innkeeper@whitebarninn.com WEBSITE www.whitebarninn.com

FOR ANYONE WHO considers the United States the land of show, where money is flaunted, this inn seems European in its understated luxury. Don't expect a water view. This member of the Relais and Châteaux group is known for its restaurant: a converted barn. Above are rough wood galleries full of antiques and bric-a-brac. Below are formal table-settings, a chic piano bar and plain, polished floor boards. At the far end, the two-storey glass window looks out onto a mini-conservatory crammed with flowers. This is a place where men wear jackets, not jeans.

Swiss-trained, British-born chef Jonathan Cartwright has an impressive reputation for signature dishes such as steamed lobster with a cognac coral sauce. He also loves to work with scallops, crab, halibut, even sea urchins. Wines come from France, California and Australia, home of Laurie Bongiorno who, with Laurie Cameron, has owned the hotel since 1988. Bedrooms range from the simpler ones in the original farmhouse to suites with fireplaces, whirlpool tubs and plush furnishings. In between are the cottagey Gatehouse rooms. There are mountain bikes; the beach is just down the road; and guests can sit in the garden 'watching the herbs grow'.

~

NEARBY water-sports, fishing, whale-watching, cycling, tennis.
LOCATION out of village; car parking
FOOD breakfast, dinner
PRICE rooms $$-$$$$ with breakfast
ROOMS 16 double; 9 suites; all have bath or shower, air-conditioning, phone, hairdrier
FACILITIES 3 dining rooms, 2 sitting rooms, garden
SMOKING no
CREDIT CARDS AE, DC, MC, V
CHILDREN over 14
DISABLED not suitable
CLOSED restaurant only, Jan
PROPRIETORS Laurie Bongiorno, Laurie Cameron

MAINE

NEW HARBOR

BRADLEY INN
~ COUNTRY INN ~

Route 130, 361 Pemaquid Point, New Harbor, ME 04554
TEL (207) 6772105 FAX (207) 6773367
E-MAIL bradley@midcoast.com WEBSITE www.bradleyinn.com

FROM ROUTE 1, the roads down the peninsula lead past open fields, small farms, and ponds set in pine woods. This is the 'Maine' many visitors dream about, far from cities, tourist attractions and outlet shopping. People who vacation here are keen on water-sports, cycling, walking … and doing nothing at all. The Bradley Inn fits this mood. It has the look of a sailing club, with models, a ship's compass set in a wooden plinth, and a 'new and correct chart of the North Sea' dated 1793. The atmosphere is casual, both in the Pub with its red mahogany and marble bar, and in the Chart Room, one of two dining rooms.

Award-winning South Texas chef Judith Carinhas is getting rave reviews for her innovative dishes featuring the best local produce. The wine list is equally impressive. The owners have created a sophisticated yet relaxed atmosphere, with a dozen bedrooms in the main house, and three more in the converted barn, where the Carriage House suite can sleep six. The little cottage is a favourite with honeymooners. Permaquid point lighthouse is only a stroll away; except for an island, you can't get more 'away from it all' than this.

~

NEARBY water-sports, fishing, cycling.
LOCATION on country road; car parking
FOOD breakfast, dinner
PRICE rooms $$-$$$ with breakfast
ROOMS 16; all have bath or shower, phone
FACILITIES 2 dining rooms, sitting room, bar; garden
SMOKING no
CREDIT CARDS AE, MC, V
CHILDREN welcome
DISABLED 2 rooms
CLOSED Jan to April
MANAGERS Beth and Warren Busteed

MAINE

PORTLAND

THE DANFORTH

~ HISTORIC HOUSE ~

163 Danforth Street, Portland, Maine 04102
TEL (207) 8798755; (800) 9916557 FAX (207) 8798754
E-MAIL danforth@maine.rr.com WEBSITE www.danforthmaine.com

PORTLAND is a small city, full of surprises. The restored waterfront is a bustling area of shops and restaurants. Higher up the hill are a fine museum of Art, the restored Public Market and the childhood home of poet Henry Wadsworth Longfellow.

Opened in 1997, this imposing 1821 mansion stands in a historic district, just a short walk or drive from all the sights. Step inside the door and it still looks like a spacious private home, with Oriental rugs on plush carpets. There are more common areas than most: a billiard room in the basement, a cupola above the roof, and at least one sitting room on each of the three floors in between. Most small inns are designed for couples on a romantic break; some cater for business folk. The Danforth is unusual in doing both, and very successfully at that. Four-poster beds, fireplaces and the option of breakfast in the room add to the romance; early morning coffee, breakfast to go and data ports appeal to executives. We were impressed by the owner, Barbara Hathaway, who is both friendly and professional. Her attention to detail is notable: confirmation of our dinner reservation came with directions to the restaurant.

~

NEARBY museums, Old Port, shops, restaurants.
LOCATION in city; own car parking
FOOD breakfast
PRICE rooms $$-$$$$
ROOMS 10 double; all have bath or shower, air-conditioning, phone, TV, radio, hairdrier **FACILITIES** dining room, 5 sitting rooms, sun porch; terrace, garden, health club pass
SMOKING no
CREDIT CARDS AE, MC, V
CHILDREN welcome
DISABLED not suitable
CLOSED Christmas **PROPRIETORS** Berlicchi family

MAINE

PORTLAND

POMEGRANATE INN

~ CITY BED-AND-BREAKFAST ~

49 Neal Street, Portland, ME 04102
TEL (207) 7721006; (800) 3560408 FAX (207) 7734426
WEBSITE www.pomegranateinn.com

NEW ENGLAND is known for its wide variety of inns, but the Pomegranate is truly one-of-a-kind. The stuccoed exterior is the only plain aspect of this 1884 house, in the city's historic West End. Inside, high ceilings provide ample space for the striking modern art: paintings, sculpture, decorated furniture and more. The owner, interior decorator Isabel Smiles, has long been a collector. Colours throughout are dramatic, from the pomegranate fabrics in the sitting room to the gold and white hallway with stairs painted to look like marble. Bedrooms are similarly bold: number 4 has big leaves and birds painted on the walls; number 2 is more subtle, in yellow and white. Even the bathrooms have artwork.

This bed-and-breakfast was one of the first to open in the city and is still going strong. The carriage house has a suite upstairs and a handicap-accessible ground floor room opening on to a small garden. Breakfast is generous, with fresh fruit and a cooked course, such as poached eggs with smoked salmon and capers or French toast. This is for sophisticated tastes, not for those looking for the cosy, old-fashioned type of inn.

~

NEARBY waterfront, museums, historic houses.
LOCATION in residential area; street parking
FOOD breakfast
PRICE rooms $$ with breakfast
ROOMS 8; all have bath or shower, phone, TV; some have radio
FACILITIES dining room, sitting room
SMOKING no
CREDIT CARDS AE, MC, V
CHILDREN over 16
DISABLED 1 adapted room
CLOSED never
PROPRIETOR Isabel Smiles

MAINE

SOUTHWEST HARBOR

KINGSLEIGH INN 1904

〜 VILLAGE BED-AND-BREAKFAST 〜

Southwest Harbor, ME 04679
TEL (207) 2445302 FAX (207) 2447691
E-MAIL relax@kingsleighinn.com WEBSITE www.kingsleighinn.com

THIS IS POPULAR with nautical types; guests are often bringing their boats to, or sailing away from, the numerous boatyards in Southwest Harbor, which, otherwise, is just a small quiet village with a few shops and restaurants.

The owners are from Boston, as you can tell by their accents. They are keen to help guests get the best out of their stay, both here and anywhere in beloved New England. Their inn is designed for relaxation and informality: only the suite has a television; no room has a phone. Decoration is cheerful and floral, without being over-decorated; 'country casual', according to one reader. A favourite is the Turret Suite, with a sitting room, a four-poster and a fireplace in the bedroom, even a telescope ready for star gazing up in the turret room. Not all the rooms overlook the harbour, so it is well worth booking a room with a view. Breakfast is Cyd's pride and joy. She rustles up everything from German eggs to a locally-smoked salmon sausage. All the quick breads are hers, as are the afternoon 'treats' waiting for walkers, bikers and skiers on their return from Acadia National Park. Unpretentious and value for money.

〜

NEARBY Acadia National Park; water-sports, whale watching.
LOCATION in village; car parking
FOOD breakfast
PRICE rooms $-$$$ with breakfast
ROOMS 7 double; 1 suite; all have bath or shower
FACILITIES dining room, 2 sitting rooms; garden
SMOKING no
CREDIT CARDS MC, V
CHILDREN over 12
DISABLED not suitable
CLOSED never
PROPRIETORS Ken and Cyd Champagne Collins

MAINE

WISCASSET

SQUIRE TARBOX

~ COUNTRY INN ~

RR2, Wiscasset, ME 04578
TEL (207) 8827693 FAX (207) 8827107
E-MAIL squiretarbox@ime.net WEBSITE www.squiretarboxinn.com

"THERE'S NOTHING NEW here but the bathrooms," Karen Mitman said as she showed us round Sam Tarbox's house, that dates from 1820. His 1832 bible lies open on a table and he would feel right at home among the hooked rugs, the understated colours and rather plain antique furniture. He would, however, have been bemused by the music box, let alone the player piano in the attached barn. Converted for humans, this has a lived-in look, with comfortable sofas and patchwork quilts for decoration. We spotted a Baltimore oriole and a rose breasted grosbeak on the deck; keen bird watchers spy on ospreys, kingfishers and, perhaps, a great blue heron in the nearby salt marsh.

Karen and Bill Mitman left jobs in one of Boston's big hotels in 1983 to create this quiet, low-key retreat. They make the chèvre from their own goats and guests are welcome to see the animals and learn about cheese-making. The cheese is served with wine in the late afternoon. Karen's quiet demeanour belies a strong sense of humour; one of her favourite bedrooms is the Pigsty. Its former occupants are long gone; now it has cheerful red wallpaper, a brass bed and views into the herb garden.

~

NEARBY bird watching; cycling; Music Box Museum.
LOCATION on Westport Island; car parking
FOOD breakfast
PRICE rooms $-$$$ with breakfast
ROOMS 9 double; 1 single; 1 family; all have bath or shower
FACILITIES 2 dining rooms, 3 sitting rooms
SMOKING restricted
CREDIT CARDS AE, MC, V
CHILDREN over 14
DISABLED not suitable
CLOSED weekdays, Nov, Dec; Jan to April
PROPRIETORS Karen and Bill Mitman

New York City

New York City

Ambassador
~ Modern hotel ~

132 West 45th Street, New York, NY 10036
Tel (212) 9217600; (800) 2428935 **Fax** (212) 7190171

Rated for its location, just off Times Square, so plenty of theatres, cinemas and restaurants within easy reach. Impersonal 'modern hotel' decoration but friendly, helpful staff. Attractive prices for functional, clean rooms; adequate bathrooms.
Food breakfast **Price** rooms $$ **Rooms** 39, all with bath or shower, air-conditioning, phone, TV, radio **Credit cards** AE, DC, MC, V **Children** welcome **Closed** never **Languages** English, French, Spanish, Hindi

New York City

Gracie Inn
~ Town house hotel ~

502 East 81st Street, New York, NY 10028 **Tel** (212) 6281700 **Fax** (212) 6286420

Modest comforts near the East River. Stencilling decorates walls and even floors; the penthouse suite has a terrace and skylight. Daniel Chappuis is always making improvements. Ask about weekly rates. Family neighbourhood; near convenient bus routes.
Food breakfast **Price** rooms $$-$$$$ with breakfast **Rooms** 2, all with bath or shower, air-conditioning, phone, TV, kitchen facilities **Credit cards** AE, DC, MC, V **Children** welcome **Closed** never **Languages** French, German, Polish, Russian, Spanish

New York City

Manhattan Seaport Suites
~ Modern hotel ~

129 Front Street, New York, NY 10005 **Tel** (212) 7420003 **Fax** (212) 7420124

One block from Wall Street, so handy for business clientele; bargain weekend rates attract families who visit Statue of Liberty and Ellis Island. Comfortable, modern suites with kitchens, in a converted warehouse. Free entry to nearby health club.
Food breakfast **Price** rooms $$-$$$$ with breakfast **Rooms** 56, all with bath or shower, air-conditioning, phone, TV, radio, hairdrier, safe **Credit cards** AE. DC, MC, V **Children** welcome **Closed** never **Languages** French, Spanish, Cantonese, Mandarin

New York City

Off Soho Suites
~ Apartment hotel ~

11 Rivington Street, New York, NY 10002 **Tel** (212) 9799815 **Fax** (212) 9799801

This is in the Bowery, traditional haunt of the homeless, but close to Chinatown and trendy SoHo. Attractive prices for simple, clean rooms with kitchens; two suitable for disabled. Fitness room and self-service laundry. Café serves breakfast
Food breakfast, lunch **Price** room only $$ **Rooms** 38, most with bath or shower, air-conditioning, phone, TV, kitchen **Credit cards** AE, MC, V **Children** welcome **Closed** never **Languages** German, Spanish, Arabic

CONNECTICUT

EAST HADDAM

BISHOPSGATE INN
∾ BED-AND-BREAKFAST INN ∾

PO BOX 290, Goodspeed Landing, East Haddam, CT 06423
TEL (860) 8731677

THEATRICAL MEMORABILIA flavour this early-19thC house, just up the hill from the Goodspeed Opera House. There are two sitting-rooms and a large garden; breakfast is served by Dan and Molly Schwartz under the kitchen's rough old beams.
FOOD breakfast **PRICE** rooms $$ with breakfast **ROOMS** 6, all with bath or shower **CREDIT CARDS** MC, V **CHILDREN** over 6 **CLOSED** never **LANGUAGES** English only

NEW CANAAN

ROGER SHERMAN INN
∾ RESTAURANT-WITH-ROOMS ∾

195 Oenoke Ridge, New Canaan, CT 06840 **TEL** (203) 9664541

WHEN YOU are this close to New York City, a black-tied maître d'hôtel and a piano player come as no surprise. Henry Prieger's elegant 1740 mansion is well-known for its French restaurant. Restrained bedroom furnishings; manicured gardens. Well-priced.
FOOD breakfast, lunch, dinner **PRICE** rooms $-$$ with breakfast **ROOMS** 11, all with bath or shower, phone, TV **CREDIT CARDS** AE, MC, V **CHILDREN** welcome **CLOSED** never **LANGUAGES** English only

NEW PRESTON

THE BOULDERS
∾ LAKESIDE INN ∾

East Shore Road, New Preston, CT 06777 **TEL** (860) 8680541

THE ADEMAS' INN has rolling lawns by Lake Waramaug, a rather formal ambience, luxurious bedrooms. The Carriage House feels more contemporary. The restaurant is popular locally, especially for summer outdoor dining. Tennis court, boats, bicycles.
FOOD breakfast, lunch (weekend), dinner **PRICE** rooms $$-$$$$ with breakfast **ROOMS** 17, all with bath or shower, air-conditioning, phone, TV, radio **CREDIT CARDS** AE, MC, V **CHILDREN** not suitable **CLOSED** never **LANGUAGES** French, German, Dutch

NEW PRESTON

HOPKINS INN
∾ RESTAURANT-WITH-ROOMS ∾

22 Hopkins Road, New Preston, CT 06777 **TEL** (860) 8687295 **FAX** (203) 8687464

BEAUTIFULLY SITED on Lake Waramaug with a vineyard next door, this square-shouldered 1847 house has twelve bedrooms; numbers 17 and 21 have lake views. The Schobers are Austrian, so is the food in their busy restaurant. Wine tastings.
FOOD breakfast, lunch (summer only), dinner **PRICE** rooms $-$$ with breakfast **ROOMS** 12, most with bath or shower **CREDIT CARDS** not accepted **CHILDREN** welcome **CLOSED** Jan to mid-March **LANGUAGES** French, German

CONNECTICUT

NORFOLK

GREENWOODS GATE
~ BED-AND-BREAKFAST ~

105 Greenwoods Road East, Norfolk, CT 06058
TEL (860) 5425439

THE SCHUMACHERS run this handsome, grey 200-year old house as a romantic getaway, right down to bathrooms which have lotions, potions, perfumes, powders and a rubber duck. Eclectic furnishings; the E J Trescott Suite is two-tiered. Expensive.
FOOD breakfast **PRICE** rooms $$$ with breakfast **ROOMS** 4, all with bath or shower **CREDIT CARDS** not accepted **CHILDREN** over 12 **CLOSED** never **LANGUAGES** English only

NORFOLK

MANOR HOUSE
~ MANSION BED-AND-BREAKFAST ~

PO Box 447, Maple Avenue, Norfolk, CT 06058
TEL (860) 542 5690 **FAX** (860) 542 5690

HANK AND DIANE Tremblay's Tudor-style house hides a surprising amount of Victoriana in north-west Connecticut's Colonial stronghold. Louis Tiffany stained glass in the dining-room; lacy white dresses hanging in the entrance and hallways
FOOD breakfast **PRICE** rooms $$-$$$ with breakfast **ROOMS** 8, all with bath or shower **CREDIT CARDS** MC, V **CHILDREN** over 12 **CLOSED** never **LANGUAGES** French, some German, Spanish

POMFRET

COBBSCROFT
~ BED-AND-BREAKFAST ~

349 Pomfret Street, Pomfret CT 06258 **TEL** (860) 9285560

PARENTS OF STUDENTS at nearby boarding schools are regulars but this is also good cycling country. The barn is a gallery for Tom McCobb's water-colours; Janet serves a full breakfast in the comfortable house where rooms are decorated with flair.
FOOD breakfast **PRICE** rooms $-$$ with breakfast **ROOMS** 4, all with bath or shower **CREDIT CARDS** MC, V **CHILDREN** over 6 **CLOSED** 2 weeks in March **LANGUAGES** Spanish

RIDGEFIELD

STONEHENGE
~ MODERN INN ~

Route 7, PO Box 667, Ridgefield, CT 06877 **TEL** (203) 4386511

TRADITIONAL IN style, this new hotel was built on the site of a popular old inn destroyed by fire. The restaurant attracts a business clientele. There is reproduction furniture in bedrooms. Outside, a pond and outdoor swimming-pool are in the grounds.
FOOD breakfast, dinner, Sunday brunch **PRICE** rooms $$-$$$ with breakfast **ROOMS** 16, all with bath or shower, air-conditioning, phone, TV **CREDIT CARDS** AE, MC, V **CHILDREN** not suitable **CLOSED** never **LANGUAGES** English only

CONNECTICUT

RIDGEFIELD

WEST LANE INN
~ GRAND BED-AND-BREAKFAST ~

22 West Lane, Ridgefield, CT 06877 **TEL** (203) 4387323

NEW YORKERS escape to this attractive small town and Maureen Mayer's home with generous porch and lawns. The formal entrance has a handsome clock; 19thC antiques abound. Bedrooms are 'cavernous'; bathrooms have heated towel rails

FOOD breakfast **PRICE** rooms $$-$$$ with breakfast **ROOMS** 20, all with bath or shower, phone, TV **CREDIT CARDS** AE, DC, MC, V **CHILDREN** not suitable **CLOSED** never **LANGUAGES** English only

STORRS

ALTNAVEIGH
~ COUNTRY INN ~

PO Box 514, 957 Storrs Road, Storrs, CT 06268 **TEL** (860) 4294490 **FAX** (203) 4290371

ALTHOUGH the Gaudette family have added a wing to this 250-year old farmhouse in the historic district of this university town, furnishings still have the feel of a simple country inn. Guests who stay the night receive a discount in the reliable restaurant.

FOOD breakfast, lunch, dinner **PRICE** rooms $ with breakfast **ROOMS** 6; 4 share bath or shower **CREDIT CARDS** AE, DC, MC, V **CHILDREN** very welcome **CLOSED** Christmas, 1 week Jan **LANGUAGES** English only

WESTPORT

INN AT NATIONAL HALL
~ LUXURY CONVERSION ~

2 Post Road West, Westport CT 06880
TEL (203) 2211351; (800) 6284255 **FAX** (203) 2210276

A 120-YR OLD mill in an urban riverside redevelopment opened as a sumptuous hotel in 1993. Elaborate stencilling, panelling, mirrors; loft-like glitzy bedrooms fit Westport's film star image. Needs more personal warmth. Highly-rated restaurant.

FOOD breakfast, lunch, dinner **PRICE** rooms $$$$ with breakfast **ROOMS** 15, all with bath or shower, air-conditioning, phone, TV **CREDIT CARDS** AE. DC, MC, V **CHILDREN** not suitable **CLOSED** never **LANGUAGES** English only

RHODE ISLAND

BLOCK ISLAND

ATLANTIC INN
～ VICTORIAN INN ～

11 Rivington Street, New York, NY 10002
TEL (401) 4665883: (800) 2247422 **FAX** (401) 4665678

SET ON TOP of a hill, with 360° views, this Victorian-style house has a large veranda and spacious lawns. Bedrooms have flowered wallpaper; corner rooms are breezier in hot weather. The restaurant has a set-price, modern American menu.

Food breakfast, dinner **Price** rooms $-$$$ with breakfast **Rooms** 21, all with bath or shower, phone **Credit cards** AE, MC, V **Children** welcome **Closed** Nov to April **Languages** English only

BLOCK ISLAND

SEA BREEZE
～ OCEAN VIEW BED-AND-BREAKFAST ～

PO Box 141, Block Island, RI 02807 **TEL** (401) 4662275; (800) 7862276

THESE COTTAGES are stylishly furnished with antiques from the island and works from Mary and Bob Newhouse's art gallery. Continental breakfast in a basket is brought to bedrooms. Half share bathrooms, so are well-priced and useful for families.

Food breakfast **Price** rooms $-$$$ with breakfast **Rooms** 10, 5 with bath or shower **Credit cards** MC, V **Children** over 5 **Closed** never **Languages** French, German, Italian, some Spanish

NEWPORT

ADMIRAL BENBOW
～ HISTORIC BED-AND-BREAKFAST ～

93 Pelham Street, Newport RI 02840 **TEL** (401) 8488000; (800) 3432863
FAX (401) 8488006

UNDER the same ownership as the Admiral Fitzroy (see p.56), with the same high standards. Built as an inn in 1855, it is up the hill from the harbour. The suite has its own kitchen; number 12 has a superb view from its own deck. Continental breakfast.

Food breakfast, afternoon snack **Price** rooms $-$$ with breakfast **Rooms** 15, all with bath and shower, air-conditioning, phone **Credit cards** AE. DC, MC, V **Children** over 12 **Closed** never **Languages** English only

NEWPORT

IVY LODGE
～ MANSION BED-AND-BREAKFAST ～

12 Clay Street, Newport, RI 02840 **TEL** (401) 8496865

ON A SIDE street, up the hill from the harbour, Maggie and Terry Moy's century-old house is worth visiting just to see the Gothic hall and staircase panelled in carved English oak. Redecorated in 1988, there are four-poster beds and large bathrooms.

Food breakfast **Price** rooms $$-$$$ with breakfast **Rooms** 8, all with bath or shower **Credit cards** AE, MC, V **Children** welcome **Closed** never **Languages** English only

RHODE ISLAND

MILL STREET INN
~ CONVERTED MILL ~

7 Mill Street, Newport, RI 02840 **TEL** (401) 8499500 **FAX** (401) 8485131

UNASHAMEDLY MODERN, this 19C mill-conversion now houses 23 plush suites, some with private decks. Old beams and brick walls blend with contemporary furnishings in cream and grey, accented by deep red, blue or black. In Historic Hill area, near waterfront.

FOOD breakfast, afternoon snack **PRICE** rooms $$-$$$$ with breakfast **ROOMS** 23, all with bath or shower, air-conditioning, phone, TV, radio **CREDIT CARDS** AE, DC, MC, V **CHILDREN** welcome **CLOSED** never **LANGUAGES** some French

SANFORD-COVELL VILLA MARINA
~ HARBOUR-SIDE BED-AND-BREAKFAST ~

72 Washington Street, Newport, RI 02840 **TEL** (401) 8470206

IN THE CUVELIER'S family for a century, this 1869-built mansion is right on Narragansett Bay, with a jetty and a swimming-pool. Like staying in a grand private house: Victorian furniture, wood panelling, dramatic frescos, continental breakfast.

FOOD breakfast **PRICE** rooms $-$$$$ with breakfast **ROOMS** 10, most with bath or shower **CREDIT CARDS** not accepted **CHILDREN** welcome **CLOSED** never **LANGUAGES** German

VICTORIAN LADIES
~ VICTORIAN BED-AND-BREAKFAST ~

63 Memorial Boulevard, Newport, RI 02840 **TEL** (401) 8499960

PRETTY FURNISHINGS in an 1840 house, renovated by Donald and Hélène O'Neil. Right on a main street, so rooms at the back are quieter. Small communal rooms, buffet breakfast with a hot dish; behind are an annexe, brick patio and private car parking.

FOOD breakfast **PRICE** rooms $$-$$$ with breakfast **ROOMS** 11, all with bath or shower, air-conditioning, TV; some phone **CREDIT CARDS** MC, V **CHILDREN** over 10 **CLOSED** never **LANGUAGES** English only

MASSACHUSETTS

BOSTON

BEACON HILL
~ BED-AND-BREAKFAST HOME ~

27 Brimmer Street, Boston, MA 02108 **TEL** (617) 5237376

THIS 1869 brick rowhouse is a traditional bed-and-breakfast: a private home. Owner Susan Butterworth is a professional caterer and cooks breakfasts to order. Bedrooms are huge; some have views over the Charles River. Easy walking to historic sites.
FOOD breakfast **PRICE** rooms $$ with breakfast **ROOMS** 3, all with bath or shower **CREDIT CARDS** not accepted **CHILDREN** very welcome **CLOSED** never **LANGUAGES** French

BOSTON

ELIOT AND PICKETT HOUSES
~ BED-AND-BREAKFAST ~

25 Beacon Street, Boston, MA 02108 **TEL** (617) 7422100 ext 679

NEXT TO THE State House and overlooking Boston Common, these adjoining 1830's town houses in the historic Beacon Hill district are run by the Unitarian church. Reproduction Victorian furnishings. Serve yourself at breakfast. Bargain value.
FOOD breakfast **PRICE** rooms $$ with breakfast **ROOMS** 20, all with bath or shower, air-conditioning, phone, radio **CREDIT CARDS** MC, V **CHILDREN** very welcome **CLOSED** 1 week Christmas **LANGUAGES** English only

BREWSTER

BREWSTER FARMHOUSE INN
~ COUNTRY BED-AND-BREAKFAST ~

716 Main Street, Brewster, MA 02631
TEL (508) 8963910; (800) 8923910 **FAX** (508) 8964232

SEEMINGLY ORDINARY, this 1850 farmhouse is now stylishly-decorated with cheerful colours and plenty of comforts. Robert Messina and Joseph Zelich added a sundeck and heated swimming-pool in the garden and created an open plan sitting and dining room.
FOOD breakfast, afternoon snack **PRICE** rooms $-$$$ with breakfast **ROOMS** 5, 4 with bath or shower, air-conditioning, phone, TV, radio **CREDIT CARDS** AE. DC, MC, V **CHILDREN** over 16 **CLOSED** Jan, Feb **LANGUAGES** English only

DEERFIELD

DEERFIELD INN
~ VILLAGE INN ~

The Street, Deerfield, MA 0142
TEL (413) 7745587; (800) 9263865 **FAX** (413) 7738712

ATMOSPHERIC at night, this historic hamlet of old houses is busy with tourists in the day. Many stop for lunch in the Sabos' well-run inn, rebuilt after a fire in 1979. Some antiques were salvaged; wheel-chair access and air-conditioning were added.
FOOD breakfast, lunch, dinner, snacks **PRICE** rooms $$ with breakfast **ROOMS** 23, all with bath or shower, air-conditioning, phone; some TV **CREDIT CARDS** AE, MC, V **CHILDREN** very welcome **CLOSED** never **LANGUAGES** English only

MASSACHUSETTS

EAST ORLEANS

PARSONAGE
~ VILLAGE BED-AND-BREAKFAST ~

202 Main Street, PO Box 1501, East Orleans, MA 02643 TEL (508) 2558217

EAST ORLEANS is a hamlet near Nauset Beach, one of Cape Cod's best. The Brownes are English, the look is tasteful, comfortable. Willow, a studio with kitchenette, is useful for families. Separate tables at breakfast; wine served in early evening by the piano.

FOOD breakfast PRICE rooms $-$$ with breakfast ROOMS 8, all with bath or shower; some air-conditioning, TV CREDIT CARDS MC, V CHILDREN over 6 CLOSED 2 weeks Jan LANGUAGES some French

LEE

CHAMBÉRY INN
~ CONVERTED SCHOOLHOUSE ~

199 Main Street, Lee MA 01238 TEL (413) 2432221; (800) 5374321 FAX (413) 2433600

JOE TOOLE moved St Mary's School one block in 1989 and converted the century-old building into a unique hotel. Guests doodle or write messages on the original blackboards. Bedrooms are huge, still with pressed-tin ceilings. Restaurant next door.

FOOD breakfast, lunch, dinner, snacks PRICE rooms $-$$$ with breakfast ROOMS 8, all with bath or shower, phone, TV CREDIT CARDS AE, MC, V CHILDREN not suitable CLOSED never LANGUAGES English only

LENOX

CANDLELIGHT INN
~ RESTAURANT-WITH-ROOMS ~

35 Walker Street, PO Box 715, Lenox, MA 01240 TEL (413) 6371555

THE MAIN draw of John Hedgecock's attractive inn is the restaurant where chef Glen Striclkling produces exciting dishes: turbot with a potato crêpe and a spinach and champagne caviar sauce. Dine outdoors in summer. Pleasant bedrooms.

FOOD breakfast, dinner PRICE rooms $-$$$ with breakfast ROOMS 8, all with bath or shower, air-conditioning CREDIT CARDS AE, MC, V CHILDREN over 10 CLOSED restaurant only, Tues off-season LANGUAGES English only

MARBLEHEAD

HARBOR LIGHT INN
~ LUXURY BED-AND-BREAKFAST ~

58 Washington Street, Marblehead, MA 01945
TEL (781) 6312186 FAX (617) 6312216

BUILT IN 1820, this house looks formal and elegant, with oriental carpets and quality reproduction furniture plus exposed beams and original internal shutters. Some bedrooms have fireplaces and whirlpool tubs. The heated swimming-pool is in the garden.

FOOD breakfast PRICE rooms $$-$$$ with breakfast ROOMS 20, all with bath or shower, air-conditioning, phone, TV; some radio CREDIT CARDS AE, MC, V CHILDREN over 5 CLOSED never LANGUAGES English only

MASSACHUSETTS

MARBLEHEAD

SPRAY CLIFF
~ BED-AND-BREAKFAST ~

25 Spray Avenue, Marblehead, MA 01945 **TEL** *(508) 7448924; (800) 6261530*

JUST ABOVE the ocean, with panoramic views. In 1992, the Pabich family (see Salem Inn, Salem) transformed a derelict house into a stylish yet simple place. Pale wood, light and airy inside, flower beds outside. Sand beach below. One bedroom has a private deck.

FOOD breakfast **PRICE** rooms $$-$$$ with breakfast **ROOMS** 7, all with bath or shower, radio **CREDIT CARDS** AE, DC, MC, V **CHILDREN** welcome **CLOSED** never **LANGUAGES** English only

MARTHA'S VINEYARD

VICTORIAN INN
~ HISTORIC BED-AND-BREAKFAST ~

24 South Water Street. Edgartown, MA 02539 **TEL** *(508) 6274784*

WHITE, with carved-wood trim, this 1820's house looks like a wedding-cake. Bedrooms can be small but are prettily-decorated. All have ceiling fans, some have balconies. Dasher is the well-trained dog of Stephen and Karyn Caliri; they took over in 1993.

FOOD breakfast **PRICE** rooms $-$$$ with breakfast **ROOMS** 14, all with bath or shower; some with air-conditioning **CREDIT CARDS** AE, MC, V **CHILDREN** over 8 **CLOSED** never **LANGUAGES** English only

NANTUCKET

CENTERBOARD GUEST HOUSE
~ ISLAND BED-AND-BREAKFAST ~

8 Chester Street, PO Box 456, Nantucket, MA 02554
TEL *(508) 2289696* **FAX** *(508) 2281957*

IN THE HISTORIC residential district. The sitting-room and breakfast-room are quite small but bedrooms are stylish with, perhaps trompe l'oeil paintings. One suite has a dramatic four-poster bed, another its own kitchen and entrance. Not cheap.

FOOD breakfast **PRICE** rooms $$-$$$$ with breakfast **ROOMS** 6, all with bath or shower, air-conditioning, phone, TV **CREDIT CARDS** AE, MC, V **CHILDREN** over 12 **CLOSED** Jan to March **LANGUAGES** Spanish

NANTUCKET

UNION STREET INN
~ COLONIAL BED-AND-BREAKFAST ~

7 Union Street, Nantucket, MA 02554 **TEL** *(508) 2289222; (800) 2255116*

THE SPARSELY-furnished look is typical Colonial, with old-fashioned latch locks, beamed ceilings, wide floorboards. Bread for ships was made in the brick oven of this 18thC house. There is a sitting room plus a dining-room added in 1994.

FOOD breakfast **PRICE** rooms $-$$$ with breakfast **ROOMS** 12, all with bath or shower; some air-conditioning, hairdriers **CREDIT CARDS** MC, V **CHILDREN** over 5 **CLOSED** Jan **LANGUAGES** English only

MASSACHUSETTS

PROVINCETOWN

CAPTAIN LYSANDER
～ TOWN BED-AND-BREAKFAST ～

96 Commercial Street, Provincetown, MA 02657
TEL (508) 4872253 **FAX** (508) 4877579

SET BACK from the one-way, residential street, with a patio at the front and a porch at the side, the look inside is spacious and modern. Built in 1852, the 14 bedrooms include 5 family rooms and four at the top that share 2 bathrooms. Well-priced.

FOOD breakfast **PRICE** rooms $-$$ with breakfast **ROOMS** 14, 10 with bath or shower; all have radio **CREDIT CARDS** MC, V **CHILDREN** welcome **CLOSED** never **LANGUAGES** English only

ROCKPORT

PLEASANT STREET INN
～ VICTORIAN BED-AND-BREAKFAST ～

17 Pleasant Street, Rockport, MA 01966 **TEL** (978) 5463915; (800) 5413915

SINCE 1985, the Norris family have been hosts in this hilltop house with views over the harbour and town. Original moulding, oak parquet floors and very steep stairs. Outside, porch and large garden. Bedroom number 7 includes another bed in turret above.

FOOD breakfast **PRICE** rooms $-$$ with breakfast **ROOMS** 8, all with bath or shower **CREDIT CARDS** MC, V **CHILDREN** over 6 **CLOSED** never **LANGUAGES** English only

SALEM

SALEM INN
～ TOWN BED-AND-BREAKFAST ～

7 Summer Street, Salem, MA 01970
TEL 978) 7410680; (800) 4462995 **FAX** (508) 7448924

ANOTHER DIANE and Richard Pabich conversion (see Spray Cliff in Marblehead). Here, three 150-year old town houses comprise a comfortable hotel with basement restaurant. On a busy street, near tourist attractions. The Kurwin recently opened as a nearby annexe.

FOOD breakfast, lunch (summer), dinner **PRICE** rooms $-$$ with breakfast **ROOMS** 21, all with bath or shower, air-conditioning, phone, TV, radio **CREDIT CARDS** AE, DC, MC, V **CHILDREN** welcome **CLOSED** never **LANGUAGES** English only

SANDWICH

ISAIAH JONES HOMESTEAD
～ VICTORIAN BED-AND-BREAKFAST ～

165 Main Street, Sandwich, MA 02563 **TEL** (508) 8889115

THE OLDEST town on Cape Cod, and closest to the mainland. Shirley Sutton filled this 1849 house with handsome Victorian antiques. The Demming Jarves room is dramatic; Lombard Jones has white wicker and chintz. Walk to museums, tennis courts.

FOOD breakfast, afternoon snack **PRICE** rooms $-$$ with breakfast **ROOMS** 5, all with bath or shower **CREDIT CARDS** AE, MC, V **CHILDREN** over 12 **CLOSED** never **LANGUAGES** English only

MASSACHUSETTS

SOUTH EGREMONT

EGREMONT INN
~ COLONIAL INN ~

Sheffield Road, South Egremont, MA 01258 **Tel** (413) 5282111

INSIDE, MASSIVE posts and beams dominate the entrance; the brick fireplace was once the blacksmith's forge. Simple bedrooms. The low-ceilinged dining room is the main attraction with New American cuisine. Swimming-pool, tennis courts.
Food breakfast, lunch, dinner, snacks **Price** rooms $-$$$$ with breakfast **Rooms** 22, all with bath or shower, air-conditioning, phone **Credit cards** MC, V **Children** welcome **Closed** never **Languages** English only

SOUTH LEE

HISTORIC MERRELL INN
~ COLONIAL INN ~

1565 Pleasant Street, South Lee, MA 01260 **Tel** (413) 2431794

THE REYNOLDS' 1794 coaching inn has authentic Colonial appeal with a two-storey front porch. The Tavern has a rare 'birdcage' bar plus pewter and plain, Shaker-style furniture. Very comfortable bedrooms, three with fireplaces. On the Housatonic River.
Food breakfast, snacks **Price** rooms $-$$ with breakfast **Rooms** 9, all with bath or shower, air-conditioning, phone **Credit cards** MC, V **Children** over 12 **Closed** never **Languages** some French, German

STOCKBRIDGE

ROEDER HOUSE
~ COUNTRY BED-AND-BREAKFAST ~

Route 183, PO Box 525, Stockbridge, MA 01262
Tel (413) 2984015 **Fax** (413) 2983413

A 1991 ADDITION adds space to the Reuss' attractive 1850's house. Diane is keen on cooking, knowledgeable about the vegetable and flower gardens, and the Audubon bird prints on walls. Antiques, four-poster beds, rural views, swimming-pool.
Food breakfast, picnics by request, barbecue dinner Fri, Sat (summer only) **Price** rooms $$-$$$ with breakfast **Rooms** 6, all with bath or shower **Credit cards** AE, MC, V **Children** over 11 **Closed** never **Languages** English only

WEST CONCORD

COLONEL ROGER BROWN HOUSE
~ BED-AND-BREAKFAST ~

Damonmill Square, Route 62, West Concord, MA 01742 **Tel** (800) 2921369

WHEN SHEILA-CARLTON took over this 1775-built house in 1993, she changed it from 'tea and scones' to 'coffee and muffins'. Small bathrooms, big bedrooms, a little noisy at the front but close to Concord's historic sites; 40 minutes from Boston.
Food breakfast **Price** rooms $ with breakfast **Rooms** 5, all with bath or shower, air-conditioning, phone, TV, radio **Credit cards** AE, DC, MC, V **Children** over 12 **Closed** never **Languages** English only

MASSACHUSETTS

WOODS HOLE

WOODS HOLE PASSAGE
∼ BED-AND-BREAKFAST ∼

186 Woods Hole Road, Woods Hole, MA 02540
TEL (508) 5489575; (800) 7908976 **FAX** (508) 5409123

A RTIST-PHOTOGRAPHER Cristina Mozo is Argentinean; she opened this converted carriage house and barn in 1991. Comfortable, contemporary furnishings; croquet in large garden; close to ferries to Martha's Vineyard and Nantucket.

FOOD breakfast **PRICE** rooms $-$$ with breakfast **ROOMS** 5, all with bath or shower **CREDIT CARDS** AE, DC, MC, V **CHILDREN** over 4 **CLOSED** never **LANGUAGES** Spanish, some German

OTHER RECOMMENDATIONS

Barnstable: Ashley Manor, 3660 Old Kings Highway, PO Box 856, Barnstable, MA 02630. Tel (508) 3628044. $$-$$$. 5 rooms plus cottage. Attractive rooms, large garden, tennis court.

Chatham: Cranberry Inn, 359 Main Street, Chatham, MA 02633. Tel (508) 945 9232; (800) 3324667. Fax (508) 9453769. $$-$$$. 18 rooms. Built as an inn in 1830; well furnished.

Great Barington: Windflower, 684 South Egremont Road, Gt Barrington, MA 01230. Tel (413) 5282720; (800) 9921993. $$-$$$. 13 rooms. Serves dinner and breakfast, swimming-pool.

Lenox: Whistler's Inn, 5 Greenwood Street, Lenox, MA 01240. Tel (413) 6370975. Fax (413) 6372190. 13 rooms. Well-travelled owner's photographs on walls. Large bedrooms.

Nantucket: 76 Main Street, Nantucket, MA 02554. Tel (508) 2282533. $-$$. 18 rooms. Large house redecorated in 1994; motel-like annex in garden useful for families with small children.

Rockport: Old Farm inn, 291 Granite St, Route 127, Pigeon Cove, Rockport, MA 01966-1028. Tel (508) 5463237. $$. 10 rooms. Near Halibut Point State Park; suitable for families.

VERMONT

CHESTER

STONE HEARTH INN
~ VILLAGE INN ~

Route 11 West, Chester, VT 05143 **TEL** *(802) 8762525*

THE STROHMEYERS' 180-year old farmhouse is popular with cyclists, hikers and cross-country skiers. Bedrooms are plain, retaining beams, pine floors and fireplaces. Dinner by request; English pub-style meals at lunch time. Down-to-earth, well priced.

FOOD breakfast, lunch, dinner, snacks **PRICE** rooms $-$$ with breakfast **ROOMS** 10, all with bath or shower, radio **CREDIT CARDS** MC, V **CHILDREN** very welcome **CLOSED** never **LANGUAGES** French, German, Dutch

DANBY

QUAIL'S NEST
~ BED-AND-BREAKFAST INN ~

PO Box 221, Main Street, Danby VT 05739 **TEL** *(802) 2935099*

GREG AND NANCY DIAZ have a hammock in the garden and a wood stove in the sitting room. Informal, unpretentious and non-smoking, this 150-year old, clapboard house stands on the edge of the Green Mountain National Forest. Inexpensive.

FOOD breakfast **PRICE** rooms $ with breakfast **ROOMS** Rooms 6, most with bath or shower **CREDIT CARDS** MC, V **CHILDREN** over 8 **CLOSED** never **LANGUAGES** English only

DORSET

INN AT WEST VIEW FARM
~ RESTAURANT INN ~

Route 30, Dorset VT 05251 **TEL** *(802) 8675715*

DOROTHY AND HELMUT STEIN own this former dairy farm, built in 1870. The Auberge dining room specializes in 'new wave' dishes but Clancy's Tavern serves snacks and light meals. Bedrooms are comfortable, if unexceptional; there is a sunroom and a porch.

FOOD breakfast, dinner **PRICE** rooms $$-$$$ with breakfast **ROOMS** 10, all with bath or shower, air-conditioning, phone **CREDIT CARDS** AE, MC, V **CHILDREN** not suitable **CLOSED** never **LANGUAGES** English only

DORSET

MARBLE WEST INN
~ COUNTRY INN ~

Damonmill Square, Route 62, West Concord, MA 01742 **TEL** *(800) 2921369*

THE PIANO IN THE MUSIC room, like the backgammon in the library are frequently used by guests, who eat dinner 'family-style' at the large table with June and Wayne Erla. Bedrooms are pleasant; two have fireplaces. Quiet setting, low-key-ambience.

FOOD breakfast, dinner **PRICE** rooms $$ with breakfast **ROOMS** 8, all with bath or shower **CREDIT CARDS** AE, MC, V **CHILDREN** over 12 **CLOSED** never **LANGUAGES** English only

VERMONT

JAMAICA

THREE MOUNTAIN INN
~ COLONIAL INN ~

Route 30, Jamaica, VT 05343 TEL (802) 8744140

CHARLES AND ELAINE MURRAY and their daughters run this 200-year old inn on the village green, close to Stratton Mountain skiing. The two dining-rooms have 'pickled' wood panelling; bedrooms are in three buildings, including a honeymoon cottage. Mainly couples.
FOOD breakfast dinner **PRICE** rooms $-$$ with breakfast **ROOMS** 15, all with bath or shower **CREDIT CARDS** AE MC, V **CHILDREN** not suitable **CLOSED** April, early Nov **LANGUAGES** Italian, some French

KILLINGTON

INN AT LONG TRAIL
~ SKI LODGE ~

Po Box 267, Route 4, Killington VT 05751 TEL (802) 7757181; (800) 3252540

BUILT IN 1938, the hand-hewn logs throughout create a dark atmosphere. The McGraths are Irish, hence the Guinness stew and noisy conviviality in the pub. For groups of skiers and hikers who don't mind the rather dated furnishings and want a bargain.
FOOD breakfast, lunch, dinner **PRICE** rooms $-$$$ with breakfast **ROOMS** 19, all with bath or shower; some TV **CREDIT CARDS** MC, V **CHILDREN** welcome **CLOSED** 3 weeks Nov; mid-April to mid-Juner **LANGUAGES** English only

LANDGROVE

McCARTNEY HOUSE
~ RESTAURANT WITH ROOMS ~

Route 11, Landgrove, VT 05148 TEL (802) 8246444;

THE ACTON FAMILY combine simple accommodation with above-average food in a popular hiking and cross-country ski area. The dining room is a bright greenhouse; the pub serves a fiery Glögg in winter; bedrooms are Scandinavian-simple. Casual atmosphere.
FOOD breakfast, lunch, dinner **PRICE** rooms $ with breakfast **ROOMS** 5, all with bath or shower **CREDIT CARDS** MC, V **CHILDREN** welcome **CLOSED** Nov (weekdays), April **LANGUAGES** English only

LUDLOW

ANDRIE ROSE
~ TOWN INN ~

13 Pleasant St, Ludlow, VT 05149
TEL (802) 2284846; (800) 2234846 FAX (802) 2287910

THE FISHERS have renovated this 1830 house with a rather cluttered Victorian look plus whirlpool tubs, VCRs and TVs. Very comfortable but verging on the precious. Overlooks Okemo ski slopes; five-course candle lit dinners on Saturdays.
FOOD breakfast, dinner (Sat only) **PRICE** rooms $$-$$$ with breakfast **ROOMS** 14, all with bath or shower **CREDIT CARDS** AE, DC, MC, V **CHILDREN** over 10 **CLOSED** never **LANGUAGES** English only**LANGUAGES** English only

VERMONT

LUDLOW

GOVERNOR'S INN
~ TOWN INN ~

86 Main Street, Ludlow, VT 05149 TEL (802) 2288830

THE MARBLE'S inn appeals to the saccharine in the American soul: waitresses in mobcaps, bedrooms with their own diaries. Their enthusiasm can be entrancing to some, overwhelming to others. Food may not always live up to expectations.
FOOD breakfast, dinner, afternoon tea PRICE rooms $$$ with breakfast ROOMS 8, all with bath or shower, air-conditioning, phone, TV, radio CREDIT CARDS MC CHILDREN not suitable CLOSED never LANGUAGES English only

MANCHESTER

INN AT MANCHESTER
~ HISTORIC HOUSE ~

Box 41, Manchester, VT 05254 TEL (802) 3621793

A RAMBLING, 19thC bed-and-breakfast, with high ceilings, oak trim and views of Mt Equinox. The Rosenbergs are courteous hosts but this is more a 'good, honest night's stay' than a special weekend spot. You can walk to some of the many shops in town.
FOOD breakfast PRICE rooms $-$$$ with breakfast ROOMS 19, all with bath or shower; some air-conditioning CREDIT CARDS AE, MC, V CHILDREN not suitable CLOSED never LANGUAGES English only

MARLBORO

COLONEL WILLIAMS TAVERN
~ FARMHOUSE INN ~

Route 9, PO Box 275, Marlboro, VT 05344 TEL (802) 2571093

THE 200-YEAR-OLD, slate-roofed farmhouse has a real country feel: use the pond to fish for trout or to ice-skate. Four suites in the Carriage House have kitchenettes for families. Mary Lou Esterley's soups are the pride of her kitchen.
FOOD breakfast, dinner, Sunday brunch PRICE rooms $$ with breakfast ROOMS 11, most with bath or shower CREDIT CARDS MC, V CHILDREN very welcome CLOSED April LANGUAGES English only

NEWFANE

WEST RIVER LODGE
~ FARMHOUSE INN ~

RR1, PO Box 693, Newfane, VT 05345 TEL (802) 3657745

THE WINNERS run an antiques business, so their simple inn is well-furnished even if only two bedrooms have private bathrooms. Many guests ride English-style at neighbouring stables. Home-cooked meals at communal table. Value for money.
FOOD breakfast, lunch, dinner, snacks PRICE rooms $ with breakfast ROOMS 8, two with bath or shower CREDIT CARDS not accepted CHILDREN very welcome CLOSED never LANGUAGES English only

VERMONT

PROCTORSVILLE

GOLDEN STAGE
∼ COUNTRY INN ∼

PO Box 218. Proctorsville, VT 05153 **TEL** (802) 226 7744

THE MODERN quilts that hang on the walls make an immediate impact at this relaxed inn between Chester and Ludlow. Kirsten Murphy bakes bread and cookies; Marcel Perret, a Swiss, cooks dinner which is included in the room rate. Value for money.

FOOD breakfast dinner **PRICE** rooms $$ with dinner and breakfast **ROOMS** 10, most with bath or shower **CREDIT CARDS** MC, V **CHILDREN** not suitable **CLOSED** Nov, April **LANGUAGES** French

WAITSFIELD

MILLBROOK
∼ COUNTRY INN ∼

RFD Box 62, Route 17, Waitsfield, VT 05673 **TEL** (802) 496 2405

THE GORMANS' old farmhouse is five minutes from the Sugarbush ski slopes. Although three bedrooms share bathrooms, the quilts, antique beds and prices more than compensate. Above-average dining includes real Indian curries. Popular with young skiers.

FOOD breakfast, dinner **PRICE** rooms $-$$ with breakfast **ROOMS** 7, 4 with bath or shower **CREDIT CARDS** AE, DC, MC, V **CHILDREN** not suitable **CLOSED** April, May, Nov **LANGUAGES** English only

WAITSFIELD

TUCKER HILL LODGE
∼ COUNTRY INN ∼

RDI, Box 147, Waitsfield, VT 05673
TEL (802) 496 3983; (800) 543 7841 **FAX** (802) 496 3032

THIS HAS ITS own clay tennis court, swimming-pool and cross-country skiing, but it is best known for its restaurant, and now, Giorgio's Italian Café. The Noaros took over late in 1992 and are slowly making improvements, with the accent on families.

FOOD Meals breakfast, dinner, Sun brunch only summer **PRICE** rooms $-$$ with breakfast **ROOMS** Rooms 22, most with bath or shower **CREDIT CARDS** AE, MC, V **CHILDREN** welcome **CLOSED** 2 weeks Nov; restaurant Mon, Tues low season **LANGUAGES** Italian

WARREN

SUGARTREE
∼ RESORT BED-AND-BREAKFAST ∼

Sugarbush Access Road, Warren, VT 05674
TEL Tel (802) 583 3211; (800) 666 8907

RIGHT AT THE FOOT of the Sugarbush ski area, Frank and Kathy Partsch have recently taken over, hoping to inject new life into the rather twee 'old ski lodge'. Much redecoration and modernising needed, but well-located for hard-core skiers.

FOOD breakfast **PRICE** rooms $ with breakfast **ROOMS** 5, all with bath or shower **CREDIT CARDS** AE, MC, V **CHILDREN** over 7 **CLOSED** 2 weeks April; 3 weeks Nov **LANGUAGES** _ English only

VERMONT

WEST DOVER

DEERFIELD INN
~ FARMHOUSE INN ~

Route 100, Box 625, West Dover, VT 05356 **TEL** (802) 464 9355; (802) 464 6333

THE TRAUTWEINS have an art gallery, so walls are covered with works by local and international artists. The little breakfast-room has some fine original millwork (woo trim); the most popular bed-room, number 5, has a canopy bed and working fireplace.

FOOD breakfast **PRICE** rooms $$ with dinner and breakfast **ROOMS** 9, all with bath or shower, TV **CREDIT CARDS** AE, MC, V **CHILDREN** over 10 **CLOSED** never **LANGUAGES** English only

WEST DOVER

WEST DOVER INN
~ COUNTRY INN ~

Box 506, West Dover, VT 05356 **TEL** Tel (802) 464 5207; (800) 732 0745

DON AND MADELINE Mitchell's small hotel has been an inn for over 100 years. The Capstone Restaurant is popular with skiers. Bedrooms are quite large with TVs hidden away. The Haystack suite has quality period furniture and a whirlpool tub. On busy Route 100.

FOOD breakfast, lunch, dinner **PRICE** rooms $$ with breakfast **ROOMS** 12, all with bath or shower, TV **CREDIT CARDS** not accepted **CHILDREN** over 8 **CLOSED** April, May **LANGUAGES** English only

WESTON

DARLING FAMILY INN
~ COUNTRY BED-AND-BREAKFAST ~

815 Route 100, Weston, VT 05161 **TEL** (802) 824 3223

JOAN AND CHAPIN Darling deliberately recreate Colonial days in this 160-year old grey clapboard house full of antiques: pewter in the dining-room, a spinet in the sitting-room. Well-priced, with outdoor swimming-pool and atmospheric, pretty bedrooms.

FOOD breakfast **PRICE** rooms $-$$ with breakfast **ROOMS** 5, all with bath or shower; 2 cottages **CREDIT CARDS** not accepted **CHILDREN** over 10 **CLOSED** never **LANGUAGES** English only

WESTON

THE JUDGE WILDER INN
~ TOWN BED-AND-BREAKFAST ~

RRI, PO Box 106-D, Weston, VT 05161 **TEL** (802) 824 8172

PAUL MAZGELIS'S 170-year old brick house sits on a hill over-looking Weston. Elegant outside, less formal inside with an appealing casual quality. Small bedrooms, pretty stencilling. Huge breakfasts may include pancakes and home-made biscuits (scones).

FOOD breakfast **PRICE** rooms $-$$ with breakfast **ROOMS** Rooms 7, most with bath or shower **CREDIT CARDS** MC, V **CHILDREN** not suitable **CLOSED** 3 weeks April **LANGUAGES** English only

New Hampshire

Chocorua

The Brass Heart Inn
~ Old farmhouse ~

Chocorua, NH 03817
Tel (603) 323 7766; (800) 446 1112 **Fax** (603) 323 7531

In the rural area between the Lakes Region and Mt Washington Valley, this pretty farmhouse has peaked dormer windows. The Staffords have a library, tap room and a dining room with a solid reputation. A bit musty in corners; standards must be maintained.

Food breakfast, dinner **Price** rooms from $$ with dinner and breakfast **Rooms** 11, Cottages 3, most with bath or shower **Credit cards** MC, V **Children** welcome **Closed** never **Languages** English only

Franconia

Sugar Hill Inn
~ Old inn ~

Route 117, Sugar Hill, Franconia, NH 03580 **Tel** (603) 823 5621; (800) 548 4748

A quiet inn with 18thC fireplaces and beams. The antiques, quilts and stencilling in the bedrooms are Barbara Quinn's choice; Jim looks after dinner, included in the price. Tea at 4pm, a piano in the pub; somewhat expensive, compared with similar inns nearby.

Food breakfast, dinner **Price** DB&B from $$ **Rooms** 14, all with bath or shower, radio **Credit cards** MC, V **Children** not suitable **Closed** never **Languages** English only

Holderness

Inn on Golden Pond
~ Country bed-and-breakfast ~

Route 3, PO Box 680, Holderness, NH 03245 **Tel** (603) 968 7269

Near Squam Lake where the film On Golden Pond was made. Bill and Bonnie Webb's 100-year old house has a long screened porch and one luxury suite, Porcupine Hollow, with a sitting room at the front of the house, the bedroom at the rear. Unpretentious.

Food breakfast **Price** rooms $-$$ with breakfast **Rooms** 9, all with bath or shower **Credit cards** AE, MC, V **Children** over 12 **Closed** never **Languages** French

Jackson

Ellis River House
~ Riverside inn ~

Route 16, Box 656, Jackson, NH 03846
Tel (603) 383 9339; (800) 233 8309 **Fax** (603) 383 4142

Despite its newish appearance, this riverside inn has some charm. Useful for families with its heated outdoor swimming pool. One room is handicapped accessible. Rooms range from 'value' (shared baths) to 'deluxe', with more comforts.

Food breakfast, dinner by request **Price** rooms $-$$$$ with breakfast **Rooms** 18, most with bath or shower, air-conditioning; some TV **Credit cards** AE, MC, V **Children** welcome **Closed** never **Languages** English only

New Hampshire

Benjamin Prescott Inn
~ Former farmhouse ~

96 Commercial Street, Provincetown, MA 02657
Tel (508) 4872253 **Fax** (508) 4877579

THE MILLERS' sturdy, square-shouldered farmhouse has a huge barn and sugar maples (still tapped for syrup) which give a real New England look. The best room is Nabby's Nook with a beautiful, hand-painted bed from the original Prescott family.

Food breakfast **Price** rooms $-$$ with breakfast **Rooms** 9, all with bath or shower **Credit cards** MC, V **Children** over 10 **Closed** never **Languages** English only

Beal House Inn
~ Restaurant with rooms ~

247 West Main Street, Littleton, NH 03561 **Tel** (603) 444 2661

LITTLETON IS NOT an attractive town but Catherine and Jean-Marie Fisher-Motheu's inn has real French cooking: lamb with garlic and red currant sauce, chocolate marquise with mint crème anglaise. Victorian-style bedrooms. Parking difficult.

Food breakfast, dinner **Price** rooms $-$$ with breakfast **Rooms** 13, all with bath or shower, phone **Credit cards** MC, V **Children** welcome **Closed** Nov, April **Languages** French

Governor's House
~ Luxury bed-and-breakfast ~

32 Miller Avenue, Portsmouth, NH 03801
Tel (603) 431 6546 **Fax** (603) 427 0803

THIS COLONIAL REVIVAL house fits in well with its well-to-do neighbours. Bedrooms are elaborate, as are bathrooms where owner Nancy Grossman hand-painted the tiles. Romantic without being overwhelming. A tennis court in the garden.

Food breakfast **Price** rooms $$ with breakfast **Rooms** 4, all with bath or shower, air-conditioning **Credit cards** MC, V **Children** not suitable **Closed** never **Languages** English only

Martin Hill Inn
~ Bed-and-breakfast inn ~

404 Islington Street, Portsmouth, NH 03801 **Tel** (603) 436 2287

JANE AND PAUL-Harnden fell in love with this inn in 1983 - and bought it. Their own antiques, especially in the dining-room, are well-chosen. best suited to couples; ten minutes from downtown. A little cramped with no sitting-room, but a long garden.

Food breakfast **Price** rooms $-$$ with breakfast **Rooms** 7, all with bath or shower, air-conditioning **Credit cards** MC, V **Children** not suitable **Closed** never **Languages** English only

NEW HAMPSHIRE

PORTSMOUTH

SISE INN
~ TOWN HOTEL ~

40 Court Street, Portsmouth, NH 03801
TEL (603) 433 1200; (800) 267 0525

TWO BLOCKS from the heart of town, this efficient 100-year old hotel is geared to business a well as leisure travel. Short on personal touch, but more atmospheric than most city hotels. Wood-panelling in entrance, pretty hotel-style bedrooms.

FOOD breakfast, snacks **PRICE** rooms $$-$$$ with breakfast **ROOMS** 34, all with bath or shower, phone, TV, radio **CREDIT CARDS** AE, DC, MC, V **CHILDREN** not suitable **CLOSED** never **LANGUAGES** French, Spanish, Danish

SNOWVILLE

SNOWVILLAGE INN
~ RURAL RETREAT ~

Snowville, NH 03849 **TEL** (603) 447 2818; (800) 447 4345

MINUTES FROM Mt Washington Valley, the Cutrones' rambling red house is on a hillside near Crystal Lake. Upstairs rooms have attractive steep-angled walls and dormer windows with fine views. Two Samoyeds and the smell of baking often fill the entrance.

FOOD breakfast, dinner **PRICE** rooms $-$$ with breakfast **ROOMS** 18, all with bath or shower **CREDIT CARDS** AE, MC, V **CHILDREN** over 7 **CLOSED** April **LANGUAGES** English only

SUGAR HILL

THE HOMESTEAD
~ BED-AND-BREAKFAST ~

Route 117, Sugar Hill, NH 03585
TEL (603) 823 5564

MOSES ALDRITCH built the house in 1802 and since then eight generations of the Hayward family have lived here. Grandma wove a rug of New Hampshire history. Old-fashioned and proud of it, so not for the demanding seekers of saunas and whirlpool tubs.

FOOD breakfast **PRICE** rooms $ with breakfast **ROOMS** 19, half with bath or shower **CREDIT CARDS** not accepted **CHILDREN** welcome **CLOSED** never **LANGUAGES** English only

SUNAPEE

SEVEN HEARTHS
~ COUNTRY BED-AND-BREAKFAST ~

Old route 11, 26 Seven Hearths Lane, Sunapee, NH 03782
TEL (603) 763 5657; (800) 237 2464

UNREMARKABLE outside but in 1992 Laraine Pedrero installed her mainly Oriental art collection of batiks, carvings and works on paper. A far cry from the usual New England decoration. There are seven hearths plus a swimming-pool. Overlooks lake.

FOOD breakfast **PRICE** rooms $$ with breakfast **ROOMS** 10, all with bath or shower, air-conditioning **CREDIT CARDS** MC, V **CHILDREN** welcome **CLOSED** never **LANGUAGES** English only

MAINE

BAR HARBOR

LEDGELAWN
~ LUXURY BED-AND-BREAKFAST ~

66 Mount Desert Street, Bar Harbor, ME 04609
TEL (207) 288 4596: **FAX** (207) 288 9968

THIS LARGE, red, 90-year old Colonial Revival summer mansion has been converted to city sophistication: bold floral wallpaper, stuffed chairs and sofas, glamorous bathrooms. There is an outdoor swimming pool. Rather staid for a seaside resort.
FOOD breakfast **PRICE** rooms $-$$$$ with breakfast **ROOMS** 28, all with bath or shower, air-conditioning, phone, TV **CREDIT CARDS** AE, MC, V **CHILDREN** welcome **CLOSED** Nov to April **LANGUAGES** English only

BATH

INN AT BATH
~ TOWN BED-AND-BREAKFAST ~

1969 Washington Street, Bath, ME 04530 **TEL** (207) 443 4294

IN THE HISTORIC district, not far from the maritime museum, this spacious 1810 house looks like an elegant private home, filled with handsome antiques by Nicholas Bayard. The Garden Room has its own entrance and is suitable for wheelchairs.
FOOD breakfast **PRICE** rooms $-$$ with breakfast **ROOMS** 6, all with bath or shower, air-conditioning, phone, TV **CREDIT CARDS** AE, MC, V **CHILDREN** welcome **CLOSED** never **LANGUAGES** English only

BOOTHBAY

KENNISTON HILL INN
~ HISTORIC BED-AND-BREAKFAST ~

Route 27, PO Box 125, Boothbay, ME 04537
TEL (207) 633 2159; (800) 992 2915

DON'T EXPECT a water view; Boothbay is just inland from Boothbay Harbor. David and Susan Straight are low-key but welcoming. The kitchen of the 18thC farmhouse is now the breakfast-sitting-room; its huge fireplace remains. Attractive bedrooms.
FOOD breakfast, afternoon snack **PRICE** rooms $-$$ with breakfast **ROOMS** 10, all with bath or shower, radio **CREDIT CARDS** MC, V **CHILDREN** over 8 **CLOSED** never **LANGUAGES** English only

BOOTHBAY HARBOR

ANCHOR WATCH
~ WATERSIDE BED-AND-BREAKFAST ~

3 Eames Road, Boothbay Harbor, ME 04538 **TEL** (207) 633 7565

DIANE CAMPBELL'S, husband owns a ferry company; bedrooms are named for ships that sailed to Monhegan Island. Not huge, but stylish and comfortable, we rate this far above others in this popular holiday spot. Whimsical stencils are a feature. Water views.
FOOD breakfast **PRICE** rooms $-$$ with breakfast **ROOMS** 4, all with bath or shower, radio; some air-conditioning **CREDIT CARDS** MC, V **CHILDREN** over 8 **CLOSED** Jan, Feb **LANGUAGES** English only

M A I N E

CAMDEN

H A R T S T O N E
~ TOWN INNT ~

41 Elm Street, Camden, ME 04843
TEL(207) 236 4259

Built in 1835 renovated in 1985 by Peter and Sunny Simmons who offer a full cooked breakfast and, with advance notice, dinner. Pretty bedrooms in the main house; two modern suites at the back have kitchenettes and are suitable for families.
FOOD breakfast, dinner by arrangement **PRICE** rooms \$-\$\$ with breakfast **ROOMS** 10, all with bath or shower, some with air-conditioning, phone, TV **CREDIT CARDS** AE, MC, V **CHILDREN** welcome **CLOSED** sometimes Nov **LANGUAGES** English only

DURHAM

B A G L E Y   H O U S E
~ COUNTRY BED-AND-BREAKFAS ~

1290 Royalsborough Road, Durham, ME 04222
TEL (207) 865 6566; (800) 765 1722 **FAX** (207) 353 5878

On a quiet, country road, surrounded by fields and woods, Sue O'Conner's 200-year old inn is just ten minutes from the busy outlet shops of Freeport. A full English-style breakfast is served in the large kitchen, with its original wood beams. Friendly, modest.
FOOD breakfast **PRICE** rooms \$-\$\$ with breakfast **ROOMS** 5, all with bath or shower **CREDIT CARDS** AE, MC, V **CHILDREN** welcome **CLOSED** never **LANGUAGES** English only

ISLESBORO

D A R K   H A R B O R   H O U S E
~ ISLAND INNT ~

2O Box 185, Isleboro, ME 04848
TEL (207) 734 6669 **FAX** (207) 734 6938

Yellow outside, posh inside with oriental carpets and polished wooden floors plus tow curving staircases in the entrance hall. White walls give a contemporary, airy feel to the sitting room. Bedrooms are plush. Water views. Ferry from Lincolnville.
FOOD breakfast, dinner **PRICE** rooms\$\$-\$\$\$\$ with breakfast **ROOMS** 10, all with bath or shower **CREDIT CARDS** MC, V **CHILDREN** over 12 **CLOSED**mid-Oct to mid-May **LANGUAGES** German

KENNEBUNKPORT

B U F F L E H E A D   C O V E
~ RIVERSIDE BED-AND-BREAKFAST ~

PO Box 499, Kennebunkport, ME 0404 **TEL** (207) 967 3879

A dirt road, off Route 35 leads through woods to Harriet and James Gott's house on the Kennebunk River. Open-plan, with a spacious, stylish, uncluttered look; pretty bedrooms have hand-painted motifs. The Hideaway, a separate cottage has its own deck.
FOOD breakfast, afternoon snack **PRICE** rooms \$\$-\$\$\$ with breakfast **ROOMS** 6, all with bath or shower **CREDIT CARDS** MC, V **CHILDREN** over 14 **CLOSED** never **LANGUAGES** some Spanish

MAINE

INN AT HARBOR HEAD
∼ WATERSIDE INN ∼

41 Pier Road, RR2, Box 1180, Kennebunkport, ME 04046
TEL(207) 967 5564 **FAX** (207) 967 8776

DAVE AND JOAN- Sutter's house on Cape Porpoise faces the water. More formal than some, with handsome antiques, posh fabrics and Joan's hand-painted murals. Some four-poster beds, whirlpool tubs. Swim from the dock, sunbathe on the deck

FOOD breakfast, afternoon snack **PRICE** rooms $$-$$$ with breakfast **ROOMS** 5, all with bath or shower, phone, radio; some air-conditioning **CREDIT CARDS** MC, V **CHILDREN** over 12 **CLOSED** 1 week Christmas **LANGUAGES** English only

YOUNGTOWN INN
∼ RESTAURANT WITH ROOM ∼

Route 52 & Youngtown Road, Lincolnville, ME 04849
TEL Tel (207) 763 4290; (800) 291 8438

THIS 1810, farmhouse is known for its restaurant. Continental classics and American ideas are blended by French-born Manuel Mercier who has two small children. Bright, fresh-looking bedrooms. Surrounded by hills; 4 miles (6km) from Camden.

FOOD breakfast, dinner **PRICE** rooms $-$$ with breakfast **ROOMS** 6, most with bath or shower **CREDIT CARDS** AE, MC, V **CHILDREN** welcome **CLOSED** Jan **LANGUAGES** French

MILL POND INN
∼ POND-SIDE BED-AND-BREAKFAST ∼

RFD 1, PO Box 245, Newcastle, ME 04553 **TEL** (207) 563 8014

SPOT BALD eagles, otters and loons on this pond connecting Damriscotta Lake and River. Canoe from the dock, sit on the deck outside the small but not cramped house. Bobby Whear is a registered guide; Sherry is welcoming with a ready laugh.

FOOD breakfast **PRICE** rooms $-$$ with breakfast **ROOMS** 7, all with bath or shower **CREDIT CARDS** not accepted **CHILDREN** over8 **CLOSED** never **LANGUAGES** English only

HARBOURSIDE INN
∼ BED-AND-BREAKFAST ∼

Northeast Harbor, ME 04662 **TEL**(207) 276 3272

SUMMER cottages have cut off the oldest hotel in town from the water and the Sweet family's inn is now hidden in trees on a hillside. Comfortable in an old-fashioned way, four of the bedrooms have kitchenettes for longer stays in their short season.

FOOD breakfast **PRICE** rooms $$ with breakfast **ROOMS** 10, all with bath or shower, air-conditioning, phone, TV, radio **CREDIT CARDS** not accepted **CHILDREN** over 10 **CLOSED** mid-Sept to mid-June **LANGUAGES** English only

MAINE

NORTHEAST HARBOR

MAISON SUISSE INN
~ FORMER SUMMER 'COTTAGE' ~

Main Street, PO Box 1090, Northeast Harbor, ME 04662
TEL (207) 276 5223; (800) 624 7668

THIS RAMBLING shingle-style house is a fine architectural reminder of late-19thC holiday homes. Rescued by David and Beth White a decade ago, they kept the original oil paintings. Still feels like a family home, though library, sitting-room and entrance hall impress
FOOD breakfast **PRICE** rooms $-$$$ with breakfast **ROOMS** 10, all with bath or shower, TV, radio **CREDIT CARDS** MC, V **CHILDREN** welcome **CLOSED** Nov to April **LANGUAGES** French

SOUTHWEST HARBOR

HARBOUR COTTAGE INN
~ BED-AND-BREAKFASTT ~

PO Box 258, Southwest Harbor, ME 04679 **TEL** (207) 244 5738

A RARITY in Maine, the Pedreschis stay open in winter for cross country skiing and hiking. Bedrooms are quite luxurious, with antiques from Ann's English family. Mike prepares complex breakfasts. Harbour view from this century-old house
FOOD breakfast, snacks **PRICE** rooms $-$$ with breakfast **ROOMS** 8, all with bath or shower, some phone, TV, radio **CREDIT CARDS** AE, MC, V **CHILDREN** over 12 **CLOSED** Nov **LANGUAGES** English only

SOUTHWEST HARBOR

ISLAND WATCH
~ BED-AND-BREAKFAST ~

Freeman Ridge Road, Southwest Harbor, ME 04679 **TEL** (207) 244 7229

THIS FEELS like an eyrie, set high on a ridge, Picture-windows look down on Southwest Harbor and across to Cadillac Island. Maxine Clark's hand-stitched quilts are a feature of the sparsely-furnished and often small bedrooms. She has two poodles.
FOOD breakfast **PRICE** rooms $-$$ with breakfast **ROOMS** 7, all with bath or shower **CREDIT CARDS** MC, V **CHILDREN** not accepted **CLOSED** Nov to April **LANGUAGES** English only

YORK

DOCKSIDE GUEST QUARTERS
~ WATERSIDE INN' ~

Harris Island, PO Box 205, York, ME 03909 **TEL** (207) 363 2868

A CAUSEWAY links Harris Island to the mainland. Two generations of the Lusty family run this complex of restaurant, modern cottages and the original house. Simple furnishings, the strong point is the location: views of the harbour and Atlantic Ocean
FOOD breakfast **PRICE** rooms $-$$; charge for breakfast **ROOMS** 21, 19 with bath or shower, radio; most TV **CREDIT CARDS** MC, V **CHILDREN** welcome **CLOSED** never **LANGUAGES** English only

MAINE

OTHER RECOMMENDATIONS

Center Lovell: Westways Inn. Route 5, PO Box 175, Center Lovell, ME 04016. Tel (207) 928 2663. $$. 7 rooms. Rural retreat on Lake Kezar. Dinner served.

Georgetown Island: Grey Havens Inn. PO Box 308, Georgetown, ME 04548. Tel (207) 371 2616 (summer), (517) 439 4115 (winter). $-$$. 14 rooms. Summer only, on island.

Kennebunkport: Maine Stay Inn & Cottages. 34 Maine St, Box 500A, Kennebunkport, ME 04046. Tel (207) 967 2117; (800) 950 2117. $$-$$$. 17 rooms. Geared to families as well as couples.

HOTEL NAMES

HOTEL NAMES

Hotel Names

HOTEL LOCATIONS

HOTEL LOCATIONS

Hotel Locations